BUSINESS AND THE BUDDHA:
DOING WELL BY DOING GOOD

PRAISE FOR LLOYD FIELD AND *BUSINESS AND THE BUDDHA*

"Lloyd is a person of extreme integrity and believes that managing in an ethical and value-based manner is not only the right thing to do, but is also good business that brings results. I can think of no better person to act as a confidante and mentor to senior leaders, who often find themselves confronting difficult organizational problems that require clear thinking, strong action, and a value-based compass."—**Dieter E. Kays,** President/CEO, FaithLife Financial

"When financial benefit takes precedence over compassion, loving kindness, sharing the joy of others, and equanimity, the unfortunate results can be predicted but are not always obvious. That is the challenge in all interpersonal relations, corporate or otherwise—to live as though this is our only life. *Business and the Buddha*'s purpose is to awaken us, and I commend Dr. Field for his success in doing so."—**Dr. A.T. Ariyaratne,** Founder, Sarvodaya Shramadana Movement

"Lloyd has had a profound and wonderful, positive effect on our ability to achieve our mission of making a difference in people's lives."—**John Colangeli,** Chief Executive Officer, Lutherwood

"*Business and the Buddha* shows us the way to apply the Buddha's message of joyfulness to the business community and help us work towards a happier family, career and life. Lloyd Field demonstrates a rare ability to apply Buddhist theories to the everyday."—**Most Eminent Venerable Master Hsing Yun, Founder,** Fo Guang Shan

BUSINESS AND THE BUDDHA

DOING WELL BY DOING GOOD

Lloyd M. Field, Ph.D.

Foreword by the Dalai Lama

Preface by Master Hsing Yun

WISDOM PUBLICATIONS • BOSTON

Wisdom Publications
199 Elm Street
Somerville MA 02144 USA
www.wisdompubs.org

Library of Congress Cataloging-in-Publication Data
Field, Lloyd M.
  Business and the Buddha : doing well by doing good / Lloyd M. Field ; foreword by the Dalai Lama ; preface by Master Hsing Yun.
    p. cm.
  Includes index.
  ISBN 0–86171–544–6 (pbk. : alk. paper)
  1. Business—Religious aspects—Buddhism. 2. Buddhism—Social aspects. I. Bstan-'dzin-rgya-mtsho, Dalai Lama XIV, 1935- II. Xingyun, da shi. III. Title.
  HF5388.F54 2007
  294.3'373—dc22
                        2007027377
Canadian Cataloging-in-Publication Data Available

Appendix III, from *The Attention Revolution* by B. Alan Wallace, is reprinted by permission of Wisdom Publications.

First Edition
11 10 09 08 07
5 4 3 2 1

Cover design by Emily Mahon.
Interior design by Gopa & Ted2, Inc. Set in Fairfield Light 11.5/17.3.

Wisdom Publications' books are printed on acid-free paper and meet the guidelines for permanence and durability of the Production Guidelines for Book Longevity of the Council on Library Resources.

Printed in the United States of America

This book was produced with Environmental Mindfulness. We have elected to print this title on 50% PCW recycled paper with no VOC inks. As a result, we have saved the following resources: 39 trees, 27 million BTUs of energy, 3,424 lbs. of greenhouse gases, 14,213 gallons of water, and 1,825 lbs. of solid waste. For more information, please visit our website, www.wisdompubs.org

To Joyce and Russell

Your unconditional love, wisdom, and support, whatever the circumstances, are the bedrock on which this book was written.

Along with the memory of Kyra, you are the Three Jewels in my life.

CONTENTS

FOREWORD

IN THE WORLD in which we all live, there is not much concern
for humane values, while a great deal depends on money and
power. Yet if human society loses the value of justice, compassion, and honesty, we will face greater difficulties in the future.
Some people may think that these ethical attitudes are not much
needed in such areas as business or politics, but I strongly dis-
agree. The quality of all our actions depends on our motivation.

From my Buddhist viewpoint all our thoughts and deeds originate in the mind. Therefore, whether or not we possess a real
appreciation of humanity, compassion, and love makes a great difference. If we have a good heart and a concern to improve human
society, whether we work in science, politics, or business, the
result will be beneficial. When we have a positive motivation our
activities can help humanity; without it they won't. For example,
in the realms of business, the pursuit of profit without consideration for potentially negative consequences can undoubtedly give
rise to feelings of great joy when it meets with success. But in the
end there could be suffering: the environment is polluted, our
unscrupulous methods drive others out of business, the weapons
we manufacture cause death and injury. These are some of the

obvious results. Because all our lives today are affected by business decisions to a greater or lesser degree, whether or not those decisions are colored by compassion takes on an important significance. What's more, although it is difficult to bring about the inner change that gives rise to compassion, it is absolutely worthwhile to try.

I am greatly encouraged when someone like Lloyd Field, who admires the fundamentally humane qualities that are the focus of the Buddha's teachings, seeks to apply them in practical ways in the modern world that can yield widespread benefit. While I am not at all interested in increasing the number of people who call themselves Buddhists, I am eager to see how Buddhist ideas can contribute to the general welfare. Therefore, I congratulate him on the efforts he has made in this book to address what he sees as the greed inherent in capitalism and the suffering it entails, to produce a more equitable model that includes the elimination of human suffering among its goals. What is now an urgent priority is that such models be put into effect.

Tenzin Gyatso
The Fourteenth Dalai Lama

PREFACE

EVEN THOUGH Buddhism and modern business enterprises may seem to belong to different scopes, ultimately they are still part of the same whole, and certain similar principles can apply. A successful entrepreneur must not only possess professional knowledge and strong work ethics, he or she must have the aspiration and spirit to establish new undertakings. To ensure a successful business, one must winnow truth from falsehood and be consistent in words and deeds. And one must have unswerving determination and be down to earth—only then will one be able to actualize one's goals in any sphere.

The ideal in Buddhism is to contribute without asking for rewards; in all activities, the Buddhist intention is to benefit all beings. Based on the wisdom of the Buddha's teaching and the spirit of selfless contribution, Buddhists are able to repay the society by creating enterprises that benefit all. If business enterprises can put aside the profit-only mentality and learn from Buddhist entrepreneurial spirit, they too will attain greater achievements and become more able to make greater contributions to the betterment of society.

Dr. Field holds a Ph.D. in Human Resource Management and has been a business consultant for more than thirty years. Senior entrepreneurs respect him for his valuable insight and contributions made to human resource management. In this book, Dr. Field uses the Four Noble Truths to analyze and reflect on the workings of the economic system. He also shows us the way to apply the Buddha's message of joyfulness to the business community and help us work toward a happier family, career, and life.

This coincides with the ideal of Humanistic Buddhism that I advocate. Humanistic Buddhism teaches the application of a transcendental spirit to handle mundane affairs; we pay special attention to the happiness and well-being of people in this present life, and in our daily lives.

Dr. Field visits the International Buddhist Progress Society in Toronto regularly to discuss the Buddha's teachings. It is indeed rare that one is able to apply Buddhist theories on everyday practice; such an equal emphasis as Dr. Field offers is commendable. Thus, I joyfully pen this preface.

Venerable Master Hsing Yun
Founder, Fo Guang Shan
Buddha's Light International Association

> "Never doubt that a small group of thoughtful
> committed citizens can change the world.
> Indeed, it is the only thing that ever has."
> MARGARET MEAD

INTRODUCTION:
IF THE BUDDHA WERE IN THE BOARDROOM

I HAVE ENCOUNTERED very little "joy" in the thousands of workplaces I have visited during my more than thirty years as a management consultant. Joy, happiness, satisfaction with one's life and career, or pleasure in the intrinsic value inherent in the work being performed: these all seem to be rare indeed. But should we reasonably have expected to find them in factories and workplaces across North America?

Joy is not a workplace requirement. It is certainly wonderful when it occurs but it is not part of any strategic business plan that I have ever reviewed. And meaningful job satisfaction as defined by employees is far too rare and elusive.

This does not mean, of course, that well-intentioned business leaders and employees prefer dissatisfaction. It means that, once we finish wishing for empowerment or satisfaction to be part of everyone's job, including our own, we face the reality that we are in the profit business, not in the employee satisfaction business. We come to this conclusion because we have not been exposed to other options or alternative ways of thinking. Most people don't look beyond our economic model—free-enterprise capitalism— to question whether it really is an acceptable and unchangeable system.

However, for a variety of personal and professional reasons, I have come to a far different conclusion. About a year after my daughter's death, a friend suggested I read a book called *The Heart of the Buddha's Teaching,* by the Vietnamese monk, the Venerable Thich Nhat Hanh. This began for me a journey, which continues to this day, into the discoveries and teachings of a man called Siddhartha Gautama, better known to us as the Buddha.

The Buddha's teachings were different from any Western philosophy I had ever discussed or read. Right from the get-go the Buddha's message acknowledged that the suffering in my life (grief, depression) and the suffering I saw in the business world were all part of the human condition. It did not matter who the leader was or what organization I consulted with, suffering was, and is, a part of life. But—and this was the revelation for me— *suffering could be overcome:* joy too could be the hallmark of our professional lives, as well our personal ones.

To bring this about, one must start with oneself—as the Buddha did—and explore the reasons for suffering and discover how to break free from its causes and end up living a joyful life. We must own our suffering as we own our joy; both are results of choices we make every moment.

Suffering is a reality—and there are ways to move beyond suffering to joy, satisfaction, and happiness supported by wisdom, ethical behavior, and compassion. I propose that we can apply the Buddha's message to our economic system and its most powerful creation: the corporation.

GLOBAL CONCERNS: WE ARE ALL SUFFERING

We are not a global society of healthy, well-fed, clothed, and educated people. Statistically, we are a society of extreme wealth, power, influence, and affluence on the one hand, and of poverty, illness, and powerlessness on the other. For every ten

Excess, and the multitude of ways that it manifests itself, has resulted in less than 20% of the world's population living on more than 80% of the planet's resources and capturing over 80% of the world's wealth. Recent data published by the World Bank confirms the magnitude of this global inequity. In the year 2000, the total population in the developing world was 5.2 billion people. Of that number, 1.2 billion lived on less than US$1.00 per day; and 2.8 billion on less than US$2.00 per day—a total of 4 billion people. The estimated population growth between 2000 and 2015 will be 1 billion more people and 97% of these will live in the developing countries. In 1960, the average income for the richest 20 countries was 15 times greater than that of the poorest 20 countries. By 2000, it was 30 times.

people living on this planet, at least nine live in poverty. The consequences of the minority's relentless pursuit of money include regional and international economic disparity, poverty, health epidemics, a threatened environment, and much more.

The behavior of governments in developed countries and executives and shareholders of transnational corporations reinforces suffering. Take the case of pharmaceutical patents. 95 percent of the people living with HIV/AIDS reside in the developing world. Their governments do not have the rights to produce generic AIDS-related drugs for their citizens. In many ways, attachments that create the unwillingness to eradicate such problems are the most insidious and deadly sickness known to humankind. Yet the antidote—loving-kindness, compassion, and generosity—is available to us in abundant supply. This is our birthright as human beings—but until we reawaken to that potential, we cannot access it.

Our attachment to consumer goods and services—which stems from our cravings and desires—is a form of suffering. This attachment negatively affects humanity every day in virtually every part of the world, in the form of debt, physical and emotional illness and addictions, poverty, ecological abuse, and war. More unrestrained acquisition never resolves the pain; it either masks or exacerbates it. The glimmer of hope, our window of opportunity, is that we as a society and everything we have created are in a *constant state of change*. We can take hold of the direction of that change.

BUDDHISM AS PART OF THE SOLUTION

Buddhism is about avoiding the extremes in our life and finding happiness, joy, and inner peace through the Middle Way. Free enterprise is about generating profits through satisfying needs (regardless of who created them) in a competitive marketplace. These two systems may seem, on first blush, irreconcilable.

Yet, through twenty-five hundred years of Buddhist history and two-and-a-half centuries of capitalism, both have shown an ability to adapt to new ideas, cultures, and nations. The Buddha's message of wisdom, morality, and compassion has proven itself remarkably adaptable. This is one reason why Buddhism, over the last five decades, has had such phenomenal growth in Europe and North America. It takes nothing away from a culture; it just adds values—personal responsibility, integrity, ethical behavior, and spirituality.

In the profit sector, the rationale has always been to earn sufficient profits to pay dividends or provide a return-on-investment to shareholders. Buddhism is certainly not opposed to this practice. Except that—and this is a significant issue—the Buddha was concerned with *how* wealth is acquired and the ways in which individuals become attached to it. Accordingly, the acquisition and distribution of wealth become crucial ethical and moral questions.

This book will offer a new approach constructed on skillful behaviors grounded in human-based intentions and values. At its core, this book will argue that we should bring a human-based values philosophy to a value-neutral economic culture. That's what *Business and the Buddha* is about: providing a needed new way of thinking by offering a humanity-based value system to traditional free enterprise.

Humanity-based thinking is not as impossible in a capitalist environment as it might sound. Cooperation may well be a viable alternative to competition. Remember, people make profits, not the other way around.

This different perspective needs people like you and me to begin an intense dialogue on resolving human suffering. If our society has the intellectual capacity and financial resources to map our DNA, create weapons of mass destruction, and explore the furthest reaches of our solar system, we can be sure that it has the capacity to address problems associated with human suffering more effectively.

Indeed, I believe that free enterprise or capitalism can *contribute* to the diminution of suffering.

BUDDHISM FOR THE BOARDROOM

It's not likely that a single corporation is going to buck the system and be the only business in its industry to start including humane values and a concern for the broader society in its business plans. However, the recent popularity of ethical stocks and "green" investments are an example of where the marketplace can cause a board of directors to re-think its corporate values. But waiting for the marketplace is not good enough. By waiting for consumer feedback to decide against using child labor to manufacture textiles, for example, corporate leaders are clearly saying that profit is their only goal.

According to the Buddha, there are three "poisons"—mind-states that are the roots of all suffering. The Three Poisons are greed, hatred, and delusion. When our intentions and behaviors are based on one or more of these poisons, the consequences will be suffering for ourselves and others.

Of course no executive or entrepreneur is intentionally setting out to cause human suffering. However, when harm is caused it almost always is a result of leaders who, in one way or another, are attached to one or more of the Three Poisons (see box).

The goal of Buddhism is liberation from suffering. To be liberated, in Buddhist terms, is to be free from our attachments to things and ideas that are impermanent. To achieve this, the Buddha prescribed an eight-step path that leads away from suffering and toward an awakening of the whole person. This Path can only be followed when we understand our intentions, thoughts, and actions.

The Buddha's teachings, the Four Noble Truths, are the model for the organization of this book. If we accept the Buddha's first premise, or First Noble Truth, that "life is full of suffering," we can understand his Second and Third Truths as logical steps on the way to finding a way out of suffering.

The Buddhist worldview is a holistic one: it finds that what relieves our suffering also relieves the suffering of others. By gradually disentangling ourselves from the Three Poisons and the excesses they bring to our practice of free enterprise, we begin to create a healthier and happier community for ourselves, our businesses, and society.

This book is for decision-makers. This book is also for those who are suffering and want a way out so they can begin to enjoy their life, family, career, and workplace to the fullest. This book is for people willing to open their minds to different ideas about how society can be structured and how organizations can be led. I invite you to be my companion on this journey through the world of business and Buddhism.

And as a quiet encouragement to make potentially challenging choices along the way, I invite you to visualize the Buddha sitting in your boardroom in quiet meditation, a symbol of wisdom, ethics, and compassion.

The Four Noble Truths are the foundation of the Buddha's teachings.

■ *First Noble Truth: suffering occurs.*

Suffering in this sense includes all unpleasant sensations and experiences—both material (a broken wrist, loss of a job, a house fire, personal bankruptcy) and mental (delusion, depression, anxiety, grief). All sufferings have a beginning and an end; they arise and pass away—in short, they are impermanent.

■ *Second Noble Truth: the cause of suffering is "clinging," "craving," or "attachment."*

This is the desire that arises through contact between our senses and an object or idea. In the Buddhist view, the body has six sense organs: eye, ear, nose, tongue, body (in terms of the sense of touch), and mind. One great craving or desire is often for a life without aging, pain, or even death, or to have the material things in our life "improve." An acknowledgment that an attachment to any idea or object causes pain is at the heart of the Second Noble Truth.

■ *Third Noble Truth: there is liberation from suffering.*

We can break free from ignorance by realizing that we cannot stop the cycle of change (or avoid death, sickness, pain, and old age) but that we can stop investing in the unrealistic outlook that brings suffering. We can do this by realizing that the accumulation of material goods and the acquisition of property (which over time will need insurance, repairs, recycling, etc.) adds nothing to our spiritual life. From a Buddhist perspective, both the attachments from which we now suffer and our liberation from the cycle of desire result from our own intentions and actions. We can do something about our actions by understanding the attachments they attract, and by appreciating karma and the Law of Cause and Effect.

■ *Fourth Noble Truth: the prescription.*
The Buddha's Fourth Noble Truth points to the way out of suffering and attachment: the Noble Eightfold Path. If we apply this prescription to every aspect of our lives, it is, according to the Buddha, the Path out of suffering. The Path is comprised of eight guiding principles. These are central to both Buddhist thought and the reconsideration of Western corporate thinking that I am encouraging. The eight "folds" of the Path are as follows:

- ▶ Skillful Understanding
- ▶ Skillful Thought
- ▶ Skillful Speech
- ▶ Skillful Actions
- ▶ Skillful Livelihood
- ▶ Skillful Effort
- ▶ Skillful Mindfulness
- ▶ Skillful Concentration

(See also Chapter 7.)

SECTION 1: SYMPTOM

Acknowledging the Problem

> "The highest use of capital is not to make more money,
> but to make money for the betterment of life."
> HENRY FORD

1

THE THREE POISONS:
WHAT'S FREE ABOUT FREE ENTERPRISE?

UNETHICAL BUSINESS PRACTICES, while, sadly, increasingly familiar, are a good example of unrestricted or unregulated free enterprise. Free enterprise *conducted to these extremes* is what needs to change.

It is in the nature of capitalists to advocate the benefits of having as few rules and regulations as possible. ("Let the market decide" is the mantra.) However, when excess occurs, we see governments conducting investigations to determine the identities of the wrongdoers and to establish new rules or apply existing ones.

Alan Greenspan, when chairman of the U.S. Federal Reserve Board, referred to the current spate of corporate corruption—Enron, WorldCom, Tyco International, etc.—as symptomatic of "infectious greed." He blamed this infectious greed for causing business executives to embellish financial statements and artificially inflate stock values. In one interview, Greenspan posited that the rapid growth of stock-market capitalization in the late 1990s created increased opportunities for avarice.

The Buddha would go even further. The corporate practices

A recent report published by the Pan-American Health Organization (part of the World Health Organization) argued "that transnational tobacco companies have engaged in active, comprehensive campaigns of deception over the last decade in Latin America and the Caribbean regarding the harmful effects of second-hand smoke and the nature of tobacco-company activities. These public relations campaigns were primarily designed to delay or avoid tobacco marketing restrictions, tax increases, and restrictions on public and workplace smoking."

The report's authors, who spent more than a year poring over more than ten thousand pages of internal company documents, concluded that the Philip Morris Company and the British American Tobacco Company (who hold the major market share in Latin America) knowingly acted to:

- Collaborate in campaigns against common threats to their industry,
- Contract with scientists to misrepresent the science linking second-hand smoking to serious illness,
- Keep secret any connection these scientists may have had with the tobacco industry,
- Design "youth smoking prevention" campaigns and programs *primarily* as public relations exercises aimed at deterring meaningful regulation of tobacco marketing,
- Increase their share of smuggling networks,
- Influence key government officials, and
- Successfully in weaken or kill tobacco control legislation in a number of countries.

that spawned such greed are not the outcome of a particular decade on the stock market, but are *endemic to free enterprise.* And the solution is not increased regulatory vigilance, but a more mindful, holistic view that rethinks the way business is practiced in the West.

THE LIMITS OF EXCESS

The connection between wealth, selfishness, and the need for greater compassion is entirely consistent with the core tenets of Buddhism. If left uncontrolled, greed will lead to avarice, hatred, aversion, and all too often war.

> "We live in a world where the richest 20 percent of the population is 60 times richer than the poorest 20 percent. This is a world where 400 multimillionaires have more wealth than half of the world's population. Our leaders have to understand that the twenty-first century cannot survive with the ethics of the twentieth century. We must all become less selfish, less contentious, and find within our souls the necessary compassion for the poorest people on the planet."
> —Oscar Arias, former president of Costa Rica and Nobel Peace Prize Laureate in 1987

The Buddha viewed greed (together with the other two poisons of hatred and delusions about reality) as one of the three primary causes of human suffering. Greed, our excessive attachment, is a characteristic that we all exhibit in knowing and unknowing ways.

One way to address the impulse toward greed is to actively practice its opposite: that is, demonstrate generosity, loving-kindness, and compassion in every action or behavior. We will explore this more in the context of *skillful intention* later in the book.

In greed we are driven by a craving or attachment: for more money, for power, for more and more material possessions, for a dogmatic grip on our ideas, opinions, thoughts. From a corporate perspective, if the focus and emphasis of a company is singularly on profit, then this bottom-line orientation will promote greed. It is not in the nature of capitalism to be satisfied with last year's numbers.

If we are to live a life of non-suffering (a joyous life), the impulses toward greed must be mediated with self-discipline, with taking responsibility for one's thoughts and actions, and persistence in following the Path out of suffering. But controlling greed is not a simple task. It is difficult to live our twenty-first-century lives without strong motivations to have more, buy more, and achieve more. In Western industrialized societies we see the genesis of this motivation as competition.

Free enterprise does not dissuade the entrepreneur from excess— arguably it promotes the idea that "more is good and even more is better." Thus the business community does not have a natural propensity to control excessive acquisition. So the only way society can say that enough is enough is via legislation, regulations, and our purchasing choices. That is, you and I must be the agents of change, once we have accepted the idea of reducing our desires and our cravings on a personal level.

There are many examples of this kind of societal intervention into free enterprise. Consider, for example, usury legislation. In Canada, it is illegal to charge more than 60% interest per annum and in the United States corporations cannot charge more than 50%. Arguably these are still extremely high rates of interest, but the point is that it was decided that modifying or regulating "unrestricted" free enterprise was in society's best interests. A boundary was established within which business could be transacted. This precedent—to place limits on interest, which in some organizations directly influences the profitability of the corporation—is evidence that *corporate excess can be (and has already been) controlled* without causing the downfall of capitalism.

Such rule changes are not easily come by. Look at how successful the lucrative tobacco industry has been at lobbying against having its products listed as narcotics or cancer-causing agents. Even massive financial penalties—another intervention into free enterprise—have not stopped the stockholders of "Big Tobacco" and their executive teams from continuing to popularize their product.

Excess is a characteristic that investors and executives bring to the corporation, and we as shareholders reinforce it when we push for ever-higher returns on our investments. What's more, this creates a *diminished* marketplace. That is, competitors, especially small and domestic companies, will be driven out of the marketplace. In turn, the marketplace will be influenced more by the corporation's "invisible hand" than by that of the consumer.

The solution to excess then is fundamentally an individual one. No solution that will have a lasting effect can be imposed externally. To attempt to impose a solution would, arguably, be another

> "I spun some yarn to sell for food
> And sold it for two silver coins.
> I put a coin in each hand
> Because I was afraid
> That if I put both together in one hand
> This great pile of wealth would hold me back."
> —Rabi'a al-Adawiyya, eighth-century Sufi poet

form of abuse. It is only by *individual intentions and actions* that greed can be skillfully addressed.

It is critical to recognize that it's not a "flawed" system or "ailing" society or "bad" corporations that are enticing and tempting us. The state of excess within which we find ourselves is about *us,* as individuals, and our own cravings. Nevertheless, excessive attachment, like any other unskillful behavior, can be turned around if we have the wisdom, generosity, and discipline to do so.

GREED

Based on the behaviors established in our Western capitalist system we, as consumers, are expected to crave for more—literally more of anything. As consumers, we continually recreate an economic system that causes suffering in order to meet our increasing needs and desires. The impulse toward greed is universally human, related in part to a hardwired need for self-preservation. But it can easily be taken to harmful extremes.

Are those who live in poverty (approximately four billion people) free from craving? In drought-ravaged countries, the starving frequently want more food, water, and aid supplies than they can use, thus depriving their neighbors. If the developed world permits this disenfranchisement to continue for generations, armed conflict, terrorism, and revolution will continue to be the outcomes. Here, greed walks hand in hand with hatred, another of the Three Poisons. Clearly if we are hungry or lack sufficient resources to earn a living then it will be much more difficult to care for ourselves and others and make a spiritual life possible.

Capitalism is based on the principle that the acquisition of material goods and/or the accumulation of wealth should be limitless. However, Buddhists would argue that the line between the excessive acquisition of things and the creation of personal or societal suffering is invisible. *Craving or desiring more, and acting on these desires, means that we, by necessity, are preventing others who are in need from having some part of what we have.* This demonstrates our attachment or our greed, causes us to suffer, and leads to the suffering of those who have much less or nothing at all.

The acts of greed or craving may lead us to jealousy, to harming others, or to having unwholesome thoughts and intentions, which even though they may not be acted upon, still leave a subtle imprint on our minds. In fact, greed can result in emotional anxieties and psychological tensions brought on by the struggle to attain what is craved, the fear of not succeeding in the attainment, and the fear of losing what has been attained. Greed ensnares us all!

Though a solution is at hand (and has been for twenty-five hundred years), we have not learned to detach ourselves from the

All actions create effects. The Buddhist term for actions and their effects is *karma*. One of the places we "see" the effect of our actions is in our own minds. Greed or unskillful actions, words, or thoughts leave an imprint on our mind, which will ripen, at some point in the future, into some form of suffering. This is called negative karma. Skillful or positive actions (generosity, loving-kindness, compassion) also leave imprints, which ripen into happiness. This is positive karma. The constant stream of unwanted experiences caused by our unskillful intentions, actions, and behaviors is called *samsara*.

Three Poisons. Why? Some have not detached from greed because their worldview only comprises the view of *unrestricted* free enterprise and other models have not been investigated or considered. For others, it is likely that the pain of suffering is not consciously felt; they have cocooned themselves in the delusion of possessions and wealth. These cravings and desires become attachments. Dissolving this glue requires us to discipline our minds.

But new choices are available to us. Although corporations are legal entities and not people, people (whether individually or collectively) create and operate corporations. It is these people who, through their personal experiences, can reshape corporations and move away from the Three Poisons.

Since each one of us is a consumer, we too can reshape corporations through our purchasing decisions. Each time we buy a product or service we are supporting a manufacturer or service provider. Each purchase reinforces corporate practices and behaviors.

Each of us needs to ask him or herself, with each purchase, "Is this really what I want to do?" We need to empower the individual because society—corporations and governments (both good examples of institutions that are highly skilled at self-preservation)—is the result of what individuals want. If we are to assist in influencing the direction of present-day free enterprise, we must fully comprehend the significance that greed plays in our society—both in the developed and developing worlds—and the role we can play in ending suffering.

THE MIDDLE WAY

The entrepreneur would argue that in the pursuit of selling goods or services there must be no predetermined or overriding limits. Limits, if any, should only be the result of how creatively and innovatively the seller designs, produces, and markets his/her products. Buyers determine the effectiveness of this process by how much or how little they purchase. If they purchase a lot, the seller becomes wealthier and the buyer presumably feels better off for having made the purchases. So the entrepreneur would argue that capitalism works without any intervention except that which the seller and buyer impose on their relationship. Under these circumstances, the idea of *excess* does not enter the picture. Wealth, for example, is not considered greed; it is the reward for being a successful businessperson or an astute trader. Wealth is the ultimate result, in capitalist terms, of having successfully used the economic system creatively.

Greed enters the discussion when we consider the extremes of *wealth acquisition*. The Buddha's teachings caution us to avoid extremes, at the peril of one's happiness, joy, and tranquillity. The overriding extreme is wanting, desiring, or demanding unfettered materialism. From a Buddhist perspective success is not necessarily wealth but is most certainly wisdom, love, and compassion. If one has wealth and is wise and compassionate, one has much to be pleased about. However, as the Buddha and countless others have discovered, people become very attached to their possessions, which can lead to hoarding, stealing, or even war in their attempt to protect their material wealth. To avoid attachments (that is, the extremes), the Buddha taught moderation, generosity, and kindness toward all living beings: the antithesis of greed or excessive acquisition.

How then can Buddhism contribute to untying the Gordian knot that binds free enterprise and human suffering? How do we as individuals arrive at a place where we see the need for balance in our own lives and see the need to compassionately end the suffering of others? As a Buddhist, I believe the answer is the Middle Way, the path between extremes such as poverty and great affluence.

In the Buddhist view, happiness in life (or the absence of suffering) begins by following a Middle Way. To follow a path between extremes means behaving "*skillfully*," applying wisdom and compassion to one's intentions and actions so that one can live one's life without the harshness of deprivation or the excesses of extreme wealth.

Such an approach creates two problems for traditional business practices: first, the goal now is happiness, not profit; and second, capitalism is not an expression of the Middle Way, but tends toward an extreme.

> "Happiness is the meaning and purpose of life,
> the whole aim and end of human existence." —Aristotle

What I am proposing is *not* to overthrow capitalism, but to expose the ways in which Buddhist thinking can ameliorate some of the more negative outcomes of free enterprise. The Buddhist Middle Way can have a very positive and progressive relationship with Western capitalism. Indeed, Buddhist philosophy is not opposed to the creation of wealth, to private ownership of property, free trade, or even to the idea of limited government intervention.

We can cause change to occur in the economic system—it is changing on its own every moment. The current direction of this change is unrestricted globalization. Why could this direction not include a factor that described "success" as the accumulation of wealth *and* the well-being of all? We can pursue financial success while at the same time acknowledging that there is suffering in the world caused by the operation of free enterprise, *and* work to do something about it.

If the Buddha were in the Boardroom today, he would teach that the real issue is not capitalism versus socialism (or Right versus Left) but *right intention*: the intention that through our actions (in business and elsewhere) we may diminish suffering and treat all beings with respect and compassion. With this intention, we aspire that all beings have access to food, water, shelter, medical care, and such other things that are our birthright. Let's begin to explore what this might mean.

"It is not capitalism but unrestrained capitalism
counterbalanced by no other system of values
that endangers democracy."
BENJAMIN R. BARBER

2

BUSINESS BEYOND PROFIT:
A VISION FOR THE FUTURE

ORGANIZATIONS reflect the intentions and values of their leadership groups. Virtually all the crises that leaders are asked to face relate, ultimately, to the accumulation and/or distribution of wealth. Leaders who put the "needs" of wealth ahead of the best interests of communities—both internal and external to the organization—risk the very health of that organization. The problems facing *unhealthy* organizations result essentially from perceptions and decisions about these singular priorities. The maxim, "It's business . . . nothing personal," sounds familiar but should ring hollow.

An unhealthy organization is one in which profit has become the sole measure of success, at any cost, and in which values and people are paid little heed. Typically, in such an organization one could expect to see low job satisfaction, diminishing quality of work output, labor grievances, poor communication, and much output lost.

If we recognize that *unrestricted* capitalism is a product of the intentions and actions of founders, owners, or boards of directors, we can recognize that *greed* plays a major part in the process. With very few exceptions, none of the corporate leaders with whom I have worked perceived themselves as greedy. Instead, most saw themselves as just competing for market share and profitability. They did not see, and frequently did not want to see, the real consequences of their actions. But so much more is possible! Those who are attached to the model of the unhealthy organization will unfortunately have to address the negative effects of their intentions and actions over time.

WE ARE ALL CONNECTED

What would you say to the notion that *each and every act in life has an effect on every other act in life*—that all of life's processes are both multifaceted and interconnected? This interconnectedness is foundational to Buddhism. Buddhism begins from a position that reality, *all reality* (even if we erroneously separate our "personal" and "business" lives), arises from and depends upon a variety of factors, both within and beyond our control. In other words, each of life's processes supports and reinforces every other life process, so that each individual is a result, and continues to be a result, of various causes and conditions. Understanding and awakening to this interconnectedness is a core understanding. A leader's skillful intentions, thoughts, and actions will bring positive consequences. Negative intentions result in hurtful causes, conditions, and consequences.

Yet intentions and the way we subsequently act on them are frequently based on our attachments. The cause of suffering is clinging—an attachment to those life processes we'd like to think of as being permanent, but which are in fact beyond our control. Our culture's fetishistic pursuit of youthfulness and materialism are just two examples. We all try to stay young—through purchases and pastimes—knowing all the while that our body is changing and our youth passing away each day. In financial terms, this clinging to permanence for greed presents itself as the illusion of never-ending growth.

The perceived social value and benefit of unlimited profit, what I am characterizing here as greed, can be seen as illusory once we understand the principles of right intentions, interconnectedness, and impermanence—most simply, that everything is changing all the time. For example, a consumer may unwisely go into debt to buy an item because a retailer goes to great lengths to loan him the money to acquire it. This begins a set of circumstances that will affect the suffering of all the parties concerned: from the growing debt of the consumer, to the impact of uncollectible accounts receivable on the retailer, to the effect of both of these on the social system that the consumer and retailer share. Thus, from the perspective of interconnection, this is an unethical business practice.

Is this notion contrary to your current business's operation? That's the point: such a perspective is only a contradiction if you measure it against our present society's definition and application of free enterprise. The Buddha's teachings are a radical shift for us in the West; if they were not two-and-a-half millennia old, I'd even say they were revolutionary.

Many of us in the business world, and particularly those who are doing or have done well financially in their careers, view free enterprise as a particularly beneficial economic system. With capital that we have personally earned or successfully invested, we have created a comfortable lifestyle for our families and ourselves. Some entrepreneurially minded individuals have started businesses for themselves and have seen their financial success soar. New products and services have come into the marketplace, customers have been satisfied, and more people have been hired. These employees have become customers and investors, and so the economic wheel continues to turn; but with both an upside and a downside.

The relationship between employers and employees is, at its core, a financial one: labor for wages. The relationship between the company and its customers is of course also a financial one. Most of the entrepreneurs with whom I've consulted would tell you that this economic equation works just fine. But this speaks only to the issue of financial gain. As employers or investors, doesn't our responsibility run deeper than an economic equation forming a "purely business" relationship?

The capitalist idea of a good business is one that earns enough profit to satisfy the owners and/or shareholders. This attitude is too narrow for a Buddhist. A good business must certainly make profit, but how this profit contributes to the betterment of the community and society is a key question that must be addressed. Shareholders and business leaders have a responsibility to create a supportive community within their organization and thereby contribute to Creating a Better Society. This is not a question of charity or philanthropy; it is a question of intention.

A VISION FOR THE FUTURE

Buddhism suggests that our business organizations adopt a different posture when viewing their Vision, Mission, and goals. This new perspective begins with the organization's key shareholders. This group might debate the question, "Are there business responsibilities beyond profit?" The ensuing discussion might revolve around questions like these:

• Is there anything wrong—unethical, immoral, or hurtful—with what we are currently doing?

• Is what happens in our community or other communities, and our reaction to it, part of our business mandate? Are we in the business of helping people and communities?

• If we are concerned with these issues, would that not mean that we have to take seriously socially active lobby groups, including unions? Would our business agenda then be, at least partially, in the hands of people not employed by our organization?

For some, a debate along these lines would again be an opportunity to affirm the sentiments of former U.S. President Calvin Coolidge, who said, "The chief business of the American people is business." Probably only a minority would assert that, in the long run, our responsibility as caring human beings overrides profit.

But think how often in the history of humankind an individual person or a single idea has changed our worldview. Think of the impact made by the Buddha, or Abraham, or Greek philosophers such as Socrates and Aristotle, or Jesus, Mohammad, and Renaissance scholars such as Erasmus and Francis Bacon, and, in our present era, by Einstein, Schweitzer, and Mother Teresa. One caring, courageous, and visionary leader (or board member) can make a difference!

As we challenge new leaders to articulate progressive visions, it is important to remember that all ideas evolve and mature over time. Capitalism and free enterprise are no exception. With this in mind, why can we not deliberately—with positive intentions, plans, and timetables—change our organizations so that they become better communities in which to conduct business?

Many of us are ready for this change. If we move, with positive intentions, to shift our view about how organizations are presently operating to how organizations *could* create good in this world while still making a *responsible* profit, we would not only change our organizations for the better, but we would also positively affect society and our daily working lives. (Of course, Buddhism does not advocate change at a revolutionary speed. It does not ask anyone to change the direction of his or her mind's thoughts until he or she has seen and understood both the rationale for, and the consequences of, doing so.)

Beyond the profit motive, entrepreneurs also must confront this question: "Are we not responsible for the people who buy our product or service, and the manner in which they use it?" According to the Buddha's teaching, *we are responsible for all our actions. If the product we make can be used to harm others, we are responsible, because we put it into the marketplace, even if our competitors already have similar products on the market.*

But what if our competitors already have a similar product on the market? Should we not get in on this and compete for our share of the market? Does competition excuse us from our responsibility? There is no rationale to justify why it would.

In 1982 the pharmaceutical company Johnson & Johnson received notice that the packaging on several shipments of one of its products, Extra Strength Tylenol, had been tampered with, and that seven people had tragically died after ingesting tablets laced with cyanide. Realizing it had limited time to act, the company decided not to make the question of how and why this happened its first priority, but rather to concentrate its efforts on immediately recalling the product from pharmacy shelves. James Burke, the chairman of the board, went on U.S. national television—all three networks—to make the announcement and to respond proactively to the anticipated consumer question. This process was consistent with the Johnson & Johnson values statement ("Our Credo"), and was certainly not motivated merely by a bottom-line mentality. Indeed, corporate share value decreased significantly the next morning.

All of this took place within twelve hours of the company's being notified of the existence of the contaminated pills. Such a prompt response was possible because Johnson & Johnson had in place a vision and a statement of corporate values that were intended to guide all corporate actions. (I know this first-hand because I worked at Johnson & Johnson at the time.)

Organizations generally evolve out of a business vision that informs how they perform a service or provide a product that will be seen as useful by customers. This business vision is supported by a set of beliefs or values, initially expressed by the founders or executive team, which are, ideally, used to validate current and future business decisions. Most organizations have published values statements under a variety of titles.

The values statement is the resource we must mine first. It has the potential to be a great agent for change—so long as it is sincerely followed and is not merely window dressing for a public relations campaign. What I am suggesting is simple and profound: that we add one additional value, the "Cause No Harm" value (see box on next page), to the corporation's existing document.

To Cause No Harm requires boards and executives to think about all the consequences of their decisions as they affect investors as well as individual employees, customers, the environment, and society. Ideally, this would create a proactive process for business decision-making and not one that involves waiting for the media to expose how a corporation has degraded its community.

Applying the concept of "Cause No Harm" may decrease a corporation's profits in the short term but it will dramatically increase its capacity to reduce suffering. *This is the missing face of humanity in the modern corporation.* Economists working in the School

> **THE "CAUSE NO HARM" VALUE**
>
> A core value of our company is to continuously be mindful of our intentions, and to contribute positively to making "better communities" among all our internal and external stakeholders. Therefore, we will not acquire any raw materials, or design, manufacture, or sell any products or services, the doing of which will be harmful to any sentient being or to the environment.

of Natural Economics have clearly shown that Causing No Harm is a way of doing business that will create a more sustainable environment for us and for future generations. (In Chapter 8, we will discuss in detail the principles underlying Natural Economics.)

Indeed, if the Buddha were in the Boardroom or at the shareholder's annual general meeting he would likely say that Causing No Harm is not a long-term business re-engineering process, but an intention requiring immediate discussion and action. Business ethics based on Buddhist principles require that once we see harm being caused, we begin to take actions to stop it! It should be noted that an ethical corporation does not base its decisions solely on what the consumer "wants" to buy or on the profitability of the product—but also on whether it causes harm and whether it betters society.

So Causing No Harm as it relates to our external customers is a significant consideration for boards of directors and executive committees. The operative question is: "Does the way in which we make money or profit override the value of Causing No Harm?" If the answer is "Yes, it does," the consequences for all those concerned will be to continue suffering individually and societally. If the answer to the question is "No, it does not," then we are on the right path.

The various benchmarks for a better society are always moving—not always progressively, but moving nonetheless. If we were to benchmark the quality of our society by how well we care for the disadvantaged, for example, we would receive a very poor mark—maybe even a failing grade. Reflect for a moment on the homeless and street kids: where would they be without the support of badly under-funded food banks and myriad volunteers and not-for-profit organizations that exist solely to help the disadvantaged? If we were to benchmark against the poverty line, the working poor, or the minimum wage, we would also get poor marks. It does not have to be this way, but for the present this is the reality.

I fervently believe that the state of our society's well-being is totally unacceptable, as we can see by these indicators. I know I am not alone in this desperate and passionate quest to have a just society as our benchmark.

SECTION 2: DIAGNOSIS

THE ECONOMICS OF SPIRITUALITY

> "To found a great empire for the sole purpose of
> raising up a people of customers may at first sight
> appear a project fit only for a nation of shopkeepers."
> ADAM SMITH

3

WHAT ABOUT ADAM SMITH?

WHY SELECT a twenty-five-hundred-year-old perspective on life as the model for this book? Simply because other concepts and their inherent values or belief systems have not worked well. The assumptions that underpin our current thinking about how economy and society function together can be seen to lead, more and more, to suffering. To make the argument that the current model is nonfunctional, I want to reconsider some of the foundational economic thinkers whose work informs our contemporary understanding of Western capitalism and free enterprise. We begin with Adam Smith.

HANDS OFF:
SMITH AND THE ORGANIZATION OF SOCIETY

Consider this essential irony: Despite the value (indeed, reverence) we place on the pursuit of individual wealth, the societal ills that result from this chase stand in stark contrast to the goals of the acknowledged first political economist. In many ways, our

Western capitalist economy is based on the original works of Adam Smith (1723–1790), and those of his peers and followers. Smith wrote at a time when Britain was empire-building and moving into the Industrial Age within a rigid class structure. This society reflected the painful gap between the privileged and the poor. Within this setting, Smith presented his moral philosophy: that the average man and woman, along with the society in which they lived, should be the primary beneficiaries of a wealthy nation.

Despite its reputation as the first major European work in political economy, *The Wealth of Nations* (published in 1776) is in fact a continuation of the moral philosophical thesis Smith began in *The Theory of Moral Sentiments* (1759). The problem to which these two books address themselves is: How have the inner struggles between the passions of man and "the invisible hand" of the market resolved themselves through human history?

The answer to this question, according to Smith, lay in the way society developed over time. He argued that there have been four main stages of organization within society (unless disrupted by wars, a lack of resources, or poor governmental policies and practices): hunting culture, nomadic agriculture, feudal farming (most clearly seen in Europe prior to the French Revolution), and what Smith called "commercial interdependence"—which was contemporary at the time of Smith's writing.

In Smith's view, specific institutions accompanied each of these stages of development. In the period of the hunter there was a scarcity of personal property, so there was little need for systems of administration or justice. With the coming of nomadic agriculture there emerged a more complex form of social life that included the idea of private property and a need for a system of law and order.

It is the very essence of Smith's argument that he advocated institutions related to law and order as an instrument for the *protection of privilege*. He wrote in *The Wealth of Nations* that, "civil government, so far as it is instituted for the security of property, is in reality instituted for the defense of the rich against the poor, or of those who have some property against those who have none at all."

Finally, Smith's fourth stage—commercial interdependence— required new institutions, such as market-driven wages and free enterprise rather than government restraints on commerce. We now know this last stage as *laissez-faire* capitalism, which Smith called "the system of perfect liberty."

In one of his lectures at Oxford he foreshadowed his future economic philosophy when he argued that the "division of labor is the great cause of the increase of public opulence, which is always proportioned to the industry of the people, and not to the quantity of gold and silver, as is foolishly imagined."

Smith's ideas about laissez-faire capitalism and the rewards of personal industry were a reaction to the commercial practices of his day. This was a time when the British government adopted the policy that the Empire's economic interests were best served by protecting domestic industries through high import tariffs and the establishment of multi-colonial monopolies (e.g., The East India Company, The Hudson's Bay Company). The government thus controlled the activities of small domestic business enterprises and international merchants (sounds like an early version of globalization). Smith was opposed to this type of government intervention. He believed that all segments of society would benefit through free economic enterprise without government protectionism.

THE INVISIBLE HAND:
COMPETITION RESTRAINS COMPASSION

In his writings, Smith spent considerable time describing the nature of commercial or economic relationships, which were governed by an "invisible hand." This dynamic accounted for the underlying orderliness in the pricing of individual commodities as well as the laws that regulated the division of the entire wealth of the nation. This orderliness was the result of the interaction between two aspects of human nature: its response to its passions and its susceptibility to reason.

As part of successful *laissez-faire* capitalism, Smith concluded that man is incapable of restraining his own passions and advocated an institutional mechanism that acts to reconcile the disruptive possibilities inherent in a blind obedience to one's own passions. This protective mechanism is *competition,* an arrangement by which one's own passionate desire of self-betterment is turned into a socially beneficial agency by pitting one person's drive for self-betterment against another's.

According to Smith, competition forces the prices of commodities down to their "natural" levels, which in turn corresponds to their cost of production. By envisioning a system of competition, both labor and capital would move from less to more profitable occupations or commercial arenas. Though not necessarily his original intention, Smith's arguments secured the status of the wealthier social classes by emphasizing the advantages of profit making and non-intervention by government in the economic activities of society.

Smith believed that labor (the men and women who work in factories) is the primary driver of economic growth. Economic growth would be accelerated when the manpower supply increased, workers were subdivided, and labor's intrinsic quality rose through the invention and use of new production equipment. As long as new ideas for profitable investment and innovation continued to spring from the worker's imagination (a precursor to the Japanese management idea of *kaizen*, see box), and free trade was permitted, economic growth would go forward. Most importantly, the general public would enjoy a higher standard of living.

Kaizen, literally "good change," is a Japanese term that can be traced back to the U.S. occupation and re-building of Japanese industry after World War II. Kaizen is seen as continuous improvement. In industry today, Kaizen connotes practicing innovative management methods. Japan has been sensitive about waste and the environment for decades due to the scarcity of land and raw materials. The philosophy of eliminating waste leading to profit through participative improvement is an integral part of the Japanese management philosophy. It is a softer, more gradual approach than the "scrap and start anew" philosophy of the traditional Western business practice.

The average citizen in the industrialized world does have a higher standard of living today than in the past. However, the price we have paid for this increase has been quite high. In the West, we have rampant crime, homelessness, and poverty, to say nothing about how indigenous peoples were treated as Europeans colonized the Americas. In less industrialized countries, these same problems exist, in greater quantities, compounded by a lack of social infrastructure, so that these problems get worse every year.

My point is to consider the reality of a higher standard of living in the West—the true "wealth of nations"—and then ask "at what price?"

SMITH RECONSIDERED

Smith believed that there should be minimal (if any) government intervention and that commerce should not be restricted by government-sponsored monopolies. In articulating his view he proposed that the economic system should be "neutral"; that is, free from intervention. He argued that if capital derived from human enterprise were re-invested into greater production and more employees, then the latter would, in turn, spend their wages and subsequently create even more wealth. Smith's "invisible hand"—the marketplace—would rationalize the economy.

Smith argued that the results of man's industry (wages and profits) would satisfy all his material needs. Indeed, his "neutral" economy, by its very nature, ignored the individual's physical, mental, and spiritual well-being. His most holistic understanding of economics in *The Wealth of Nations* came when he noted that the division of labor (anticipating the modern assembly line) could rob workers of their intelligence and spirit: "The man whose whole life is spent in performing a few simple operations, of which the effects too are, perhaps, always the same, has no occasion to exert his understanding, or to exercise his invention in finding out expedients to remove difficulties. He, naturally, therefore loses the habit of such exertion, and generally becomes as stupid and ignorant as it is possible for a human creature to become."

To remedy this dullness, Smith supported publicly funded education. While this is as close as Smith came to a "holistic" economic view, by and large Smith failed to understand that economic relationships cannot be neutral, that indeed they *must* have a human face.

In *The Wealth of Nations,* Smith sets out the parameters of economic self-interest: "Every man, as long as he does not violate the laws of justice, is left perfectly free to pursue his own interest his own way, and to bring both his industry and capital into competition with any other man, or order of men."

When Smith wrote the *Wealth of Nations,* the English legal system had been flourishing for over five hundred years, but Smith chose to make reference to the "law of justice" and not the "law of the land." The law of justice is based on fairness or moral rightness (a key tenet in Buddhism) and is regrettably open to interpretation. It is this fact that gets some business leaders into trouble.

Smith favored "enlightened" self-interest. He believed firmly that a free commercial society actually moderates human passions and prevents a descent into a pre-civilized existence. He argued that commerce encourages people to defer gratification and to become educated, industrious, and self-disciplined. It is, he argues, the fear of losing customers "which restrains [the entrepreneur's] frauds and corrects his negligence."

The Buddha would find nothing unskillful about hard work, industrious and self-disciplined behavior, and the pursuit of an education. While Smith would direct these qualities toward the creation of wealth, the Buddhist would pursue the attainment of wisdom, ethical behavior, and compassion—in sum, of freedom from suffering. The difference lies in the intention one has in developing these qualities.

And what are the intentions of unrestricted free enterprise? As Joanna Macy argues in *Dharma and Development,* the West's dependence on a continual consumption of non-renewable resources is unsustainable: "It cannot last, for the simple reason that it is inexorably and exponentially destroying itself."

I do not believe this is what Adam Smith intended.

MR. SMITH CERTAINLY WENT TO WASHINGTON

Few theoretical concepts ever become entrenched without being altered over time by people and events. In attempting to maintain their assumptions about economic neutrality, economists have often understood Smith's arguments as immune from any moral, ethical, or religious code. And indeed, free enterprise, as it has evolved since *The Wealth of Nations* was published, has neither embraced the concept of interconnectedness nor adopted an ethical code.

Sadly, today we are faced with the results of such omissions.

It is time to reexamine the value we place on competitiveness and the survival of the fiscally fittest. Although generosity, compassion, and aid to the poor are core components of the Jewish, Christian, and Islamic codes of behavior, the Western world, in the last two to three hundred years, has allowed a system of commerce (and its resultant management and administrative structures) to develop and prosper in isolation, without guidance from its powerful religious and philosophical traditions.

The prosperity our free-enterprise system has achieved is without an apparent proportional enhancement to the spiritual lives of our citizens and the betterment of our environment. The current state of Western society compels us to call into question contemporary economic thought. Most economists, although acutely aware of the current crises, still believe that solutions to our problems can be found within conventional wisdom. But we must ask whether this wisdom, based on Adam Smith's 230-year-old theoretical constructs, is now obsolete.

> "Economics that hurt the moral well-being of an individual
> or a nation are immoral and therefore sinful."
> MAHATMA GANDHI

4

THE GROWTH FETISH:
WHO SAYS SIZE MATTERS?

TRADITIONAL economic analysis privileges acquisition, material wealth, expansion, competition, and what might now be seen as an obsession with technology. In short, growth at almost any cost—including destruction of the environment and even war.

Perhaps nothing is more revealing of the dark side of free enterprise than war. There is no question that many international aggressions have been motivated by economic considerations, from European empire-building between the fifteenth and nineteenth centuries, to the Nazi invasion of the Soviet Union during the Second World War.

Military free enterprise, first brought into the White House, and especially into the Pentagon, in relatively low-budget investments during the Vietnam war, can presently be seen in the Bush administration's push to privatize the Iraq war. For-profit military companies earn an estimated $100 billion in business worldwide each year, with much of the money going to Fortune 500 firms like Halliburton, DynCorp, Lockheed Martin, and Raytheon.

Many recent critics have accused the George W. Bush administration of cloaking its desire to control Iraqi oil in the shroud of a "war on terror." And, on the balance sheet, war results in increased trade, higher employment, innovation in a variety of technical fields, and the movement of vast amounts of capital.

The unrestricted nature of capitalism, which acts as the basis for such conflicts, encourages the excess and greed that the Buddha saw as the cause of suffering.

By feeding its obsession with economic growth, our Western society has, in its extremes, encouraged the pursuit of goals that are both unethical and dangerous. Most of us recognize these disadvantages. But how did we get here?

"LINEAR" ECONOMICS AND OUR FASCINATION WITH GROWTH

Much of our current economic thinking has its roots in the work of seventeenth-century French philosopher René Descartes and his followers. One of the central tenets of their philosophy was the belief that the human mind is an entity entirely separate from the body. At the time, this was revolutionary thinking, and it firmly planted the mind-body split within Western philosophic traditions.

This seemingly simple notion has profound implications. It leads to the conclusion that the needs of the body are somehow separate and distinct from the needs of the mind, and that these can be satisfied in different ways. This one idea crystallizes a significant difference between Western and Eastern philosophies. In Buddhism, there is a direct mind-body connection; and it is precisely this connection that I'm proposing is missing from today's "linear" thinking about economics.

I use the world "linear"—literally meaning a straight line—to distinguish narrow, unidirectional thinking from "holistic" thinking, which takes into consideration the totality of a person's needs. Linear economic thinking expresses the view that commerce is based solely on factors such as consumption, worth to the purchaser, price, and utility.

John Maynard Keynes, working within this framework of linear economics, introduced a major paradigm shift in capitalist economic thought in his 1936 opus, *The General Theory of Employment, Interest and Money*. Keynes shifted the thinking from the micro-level, and a focus on how markets are cleared and balanced, to the macro-level—the study of economic components such as the interrelationships of GNP (Gross National Product), interest rates, the quantity of money made available by a central bank, and employment.

While built upon the foundation laid by Adam Smith, Keynes argued (unlike Smith) that it was through central institutions, like banks and government, that macro-economic variables could be adjusted to achieve greater employment and increased production. In his words, "Man, in the pursuit of his self-interest, would achieve through the mechanism of the market the optimal level of activity, and therefore satisfaction for society."

Written during and to address the hardships of the Great Depression, the *General Theory* argued that it was necessary to keep people producing and consuming. Continued economic *growth* was the generator that would turn around the engine of the economy and ensure future well-being—a notion which reinforced the view that material wealth and well-being are one and the same. For Keynes, as for Smith before him, human values played no part in economic models. This exposes one of the fundamental shortcomings of traditional free-enterprise economic analysis: its inability to holistically grasp the effects of the unfettered pursuit of economic growth.

The fallacy in our fascination with growth is the erroneous belief that everyone benefits from growth. Take, for example, one of the underlying principles in free enterprise: that the more wealth a business creates, the more wealth will be invested in systems and technologies to operate the business more efficiently and effectively. According to Adam Smith, this will create more wealth for both employees and entrepreneurs. In the vast majority of business cases, however, this is *not* what has happened. What we see historically is that where low wages can be paid, they are.

All North American and European jurisdictions have employment requirements concerning a minimum hourly rate. This is because there have been too many cases where employers have paid employees unconscionably low wages. You will find numerous businesses, as well as trade and manufacturing associations, standing opposed to any increase in the minimum wage. If their lobbying efforts do not succeed, work is frequently taken offshore, where wages are, all too often, not regulated by legislation (the textile industry in less developed countries is a high-profile example). Since wages are the measure of the quality of one's basic needs, those who control payroll inevitably control the future of millions of people on this planet. They are also the same people who propel our fascination with economic growth.

ECONOMIC GROWTH: WHO BENEFITS?

There are several key points to be made regarding the traditional view of economic growth:

Most economists believe that growth is the only tool available to allow wealth to "trickle down" to the poor. In spite of the demonstrable failure of this thinking, and in spite of growth having failed to improve the lot of the average person in most countries, the current economic models are still not able to deal with the growth issue either qualitatively or systemically. The danger is in embracing unqualified growth, since it inevitably leads to the depletion of the earth's natural resources.

It naturally follows that any economic model that does not (1) require the slowing down or stopping of natural resource depletion, (2) advocate a renewal and recycling of resources as happens in the rest of nature, and (3) propose limitations on the explosion in population *cannot* be seriously regarded as a viable solution in helping to deal with humankind's immediate and most urgent concerns.

For example, one of the key reasons for the global population crisis is that many people (particularly in less developed countries) attempt to secure their old age through having enough children to support them. This immediately compounds their often already burdensome poverty. However, a small increase in government financial support, mixed with the security of savings that can be applied to non-taxable income in old age, might well reverse the need for this population growth. Yet, many governments, as well as national and international institutions, fail to recognize the apparent logic of this political and social reality and continue to advocate old solutions to tackle an issue of such global importance.

Another troubling aspect of the growth fetish is our culture's fascination with technological growth, specifically machines, gadgets, and weapons of war. This frequently leads to needless and sometimes absurd consumption and a technological displacement of employees with little thought to their future needs or well-being. There is also an increasing global stockpile of dangerous armaments

> Humankind has been around for about 100,000 years, yet it will take 500,000 years for weapons-grade plutonium to degrade.

and environmentally non-viable, energy-consuming technologies.

Continued economic growth is also characterized by institutions that continue to apply traditional economic concepts and tools. Large institutions (governments, banks, transnational corporations, etc.), after achieving a certain size, become overly focused on self-preservation, distorting the original purpose of their creation and thereby adding to the mass of social problems rather than contributing to a solution. In management terms, this inertia spawns *silos* (see box).

Large organizations over time have a tendency to be comprised by a series of sizeable "mini-organizations." As a whole, the organization becomes inflexible, less adaptable, and driven by self-interest. In short, it becomes less of an integrated, holistic environment.

The primacy of growth has resulted in very few laws to control the spread and influence of global or transnational corporations. Many of these international corporations are profitable because of their very specialization and their isolation (or protection) from local or domestic economic pressures. For example, an American corporation operating in Thailand has no obligation to adhere to the values, culture, policies, and practices in place at its parent company in the United States.

Silo is a term used in both organizational design and financial budgeting to represent keeping something separate or compartmentalized. A department that is "siloed" is one that operates on its own, is territorial, and misses the synergy that comes from acting with other departments and relationships within the organization as a whole.

I consulted for one particular company that had silos throughout its organization. Self-interest and turf protection, both personal and departmental, were entrenched in its culture. The finance department never worked with the sales department (who thought of themselves as the grandest silo of them all). Once a month all the department managers got together, had lunch, and yelled at each other. This was supposedly their leadership update meeting. They held the meeting off-site so that their employees would not hear them screaming. This type of behavior was systemic and represented individual and departmental self-interest overtaking corporate goals.

NATURAL ECONOMICS

Adam Smith pointed the way to a free-enterprise system intended to provide economic opportunity for all. John Maynard Keynes suggested that the management tools for such an economy would be large enterprises, institutions, and governments, with business growth as the bedrock of financial survival. So the natural pattern for any corporation to follow would be that of growth—with as few limitations as possible.

Today, more and more economists are beginning to challenge this thinking. This reconsideration has been championed by proponents of the School of Natural Economics, including Paul Hawkens, Amory Lovins, Hunter Lovins, and Fritjof Capra. They argue that the Keynesian model has become obsolete.

Natural Economics has evolved out of the dissatisfaction with Adam Smith's interpretation and application of the *Wealth of Nations*. Major steps were made by the philosopher Fritjof Capra *(The Turning Point: Science, Society and the Rising Culture)* who argued that all thinking is based on one's view of the subject. He used Einstein, Newton, and Galileo as examples of creative minds who changed their "paradigm" and saw the world differently. In the 1950s and '60s economists like Paul Hawkens, Amory Lovins, and others began to argue that the values underpinning present-day (unrestricted) capitalism were, at their base, a belief that the more money one had, the more things of value one could buy, and that this would lead to a greater sense of well-being. However, this view totally disregards the human, social, and ecological environments. Natural Economics does not start with money or capital but with human well-being, social relationships, our ability to meet our needs, our connection with the environment, and our need for spiritual meaning. The whole Corporate Social Responsibility and Triple Bottom-Line movement has its origin in Natural Economics.

If the Western economic system, arguably with the weight of history working in its favor, is still encouraging wealthy nations to spend more on military endeavors than on solving social issues (poverty, health care, education), perhaps we should look to other sources for ideas and inspiration for Creating a Better Society, to help us transition from the framework of the creation of wealth as the sole metric of success, to one in which we are concerned about how wealth is earned and how it is subsequently distributed.

> "The Keynesian model has now become inappropriate because it ignores so many factors that are crucial to understanding the economic situation. It concentrates on the domestic economy, dissociating it from the global economic network and disregarding international economic agreements; it neglects the overwhelming political power of transnational corporations, pays no attention to political conditions, and ignores the social and environmental costs of economic activities. At best the Keynesian approach can provide a set of possible scenarios but cannot make specific predictions. Like most traditional or linear economic thought, it has outlived its usefulness." —Fritjof Capra

The transition will most easily happen if the most influential and powerful individuals and groups in our society are willing to participate—yet every contribution is important. What's more, it can be seen to be taking place in other aspects of our lives. In psychology and medicine, there has been a shift away from traditional linear approaches to more holistic and ecological visions. Traditional economists and business strategists must follow suit, re-evaluating their conceptual frameworks and re-designing their basic models and theories accordingly.

In *The Turning Point,* Fritjof Capra offers one example of how traditional thinking must change, when he notes: "There is a tremendous need for simple skills like carpentry, plumbing, child-care, and all kinds of repair and maintenance jobs, which have been socially devalued and severely neglected, although they continue to be as important as ever. Instead of learning new skills and becoming self-sufficient, most employees remain totally dependent on large corporate institutions and, in times of economic hardship, see no other alternative than collecting unemployment

> "What the two hands of the laborer could achieve, the capitalist would never get with all his gold and silver." —Mahatma Gandhi

checks and accepting passively (though erroneously) that the situation is beyond their control."

Additionally, many Natural Economists are calling for a redefinition of "work," as we know it today. They argue that traditional definitions of work are limited solely to measurements of its contribution to a country's GNP. Such a perspective only captures the *economic* value of work—there is no assessment of the work's contribution to *human values.* Moreover, some suggest that work that produces weapons of war needs to be viewed as inherently wrong and ruinous to the spiritual and physical well-being of individuals and society.

Seen from a Buddhist vantage point, the work whose results disappear the fastest and are often valued the least by current societal measures is frequently quite necessary to the human condition. An example would be healthcare work that contributes (albeit indirectly) to individual patient care: hospital housekeeping, maintenance, food preparation, entry-level nursing staff, pastoral care, etc. These jobs are compensated for and valued—according to dollars and cents—far less than primary medical staff, but they are no less essential to the provision of adequate healthcare.

> "Ordinary work, as the root meaning of the term indicates, is work that is in harmony with the order we perceive in the natural environment." —Fritjof Capra

On the other hand, high job status is generally attached to highly technical and lasting product work, such as the building of skyscrapers, computer networks, or nuclear warheads. The administration of such highly technical enterprises is also highly regarded. Not surprisingly, these jobs are also highly paid. We should not, however, lose sight of the fact that such a hierarchy of work is not holistic and has no basis in either Eastern or Western spiritual traditions.

5

EVERYTHING'S LOCAL
IN THE GLOBAL ECONOMY

THE EVIDENCE of globalization—the spread of transnational corporate interests subsuming local businesses—is all around us. And while writers and activists such as Noam Chomsky and Naomi Klein have railed against this phenomenon, there have been no signs that it is slowing down.

Globalization is sometimes sold as a means to extend economic wealth and democracy throughout the developing world. The reality, however, has not lived up to the promise.

Yet we are not without hope or solutions. Indeed, in its 2004 report, Worldwatch Institute suggested four ways in which governments, businesses, and consumers could re-direct consumption for the benefit of all society:

▶ *Ecological Tax Reform.* By shifting taxes so that manufacturers have to pay for the harm they do to the environment, and by introducing production standards and other regulatory

> ■ The total sales of the top 200 transnational corporations are greater than the combined Gross Domestic Product (GDP) of 182 countries. Only the nine wealthiest nations in the world can compete with the global influence of the corporation.
>
> ■ According to Sarah Anderson and John Cavanagh of the Institute for Policy Studies, only 49 of the 100 largest economies in the world are nation states—the rest are transnational corporations.

tools, governments can help minimize negative impacts on natural resources.

▶ *Take-Back Laws.* Now being adopted by a growing number of governments around the world, these laws require companies to take back products at the end of their useful lives, and typically ban the disposal of products in landfills or through incineration.

▶ *Durability.* Industries can take shared responsibility for their ecological impacts by finding ways to reduce the amount of raw materials needed to create products and by making goods more durable and easy to repair and upgrade.

▶ *Personal Responsibility.* Changes in consumption practices will also require millions of individual decisions that start at the grassroots—about everything from our use of energy and water to our consumption of food.

Two hundred and fifty years of Adam Smith's legacy seems a tall order to change. The solution, from a Buddhist perspective, is to

> "While globalization has created unprecedented riches, many people have also been left mired in poverty. Industrialized countries with developed infrastructure, institutions and education, and middle-income countries, which opened up their economy, have benefited most from globalization, but the poorest countries have not grown, or in some cases have sunk back. Thus despite the overall fall in the rate of poverty, close to a third of the world population still lives in utter poverty without access to electricity or drinking water. The gap between the rich and the poor countries and between the wealthy and the indigent within countries has also widened." —Nayan Chanda

understand the nature of suffering—that our life is full of choices and each and every choice will have different consequences, and that we are responsible for our own intentions, actions, and behaviors. And how much longer can we stomach the alternative? As a society we must aspire to more. We can and must do better.

GOING GLOBAL

At its most fundamental level, business growth is reflected in the bottom line. The pursuit of growth leads corporations to market products and services wherever they can be sold. Most executives realize that geographic boundaries are invisible unless governments erect "stop" signs. And the greater the pressure for continent-wide and worldwide free-trade agreements, the quicker the boundaries disappear.

Without "do not enter" legislation—to preserve, for example,

> "A billion hours ago human life appeared on earth. A billion
> minutes ago Christianity emerged. A billion Coca-Colas was
> yesterday morning. What must we do to make a billion Coca-
> Colas this morning?"
> —from the 1996 annual report of The Coca-Cola Company

indigenous cultures and non-technological ways of working—
corporations will gravitate to virtually any marketplace. Executives will assess the risk against numerous factors:

▶ Has the new marketplace already expressed a need for this
  product?
▶ What is the likelihood of persuading (through advertising
  and public relations) the market that there is a need for this
  product?
▶ Will operating costs (e.g., the labor rate) be low enough to
  use this market as a source for production capacity?

The boardroom discussion will also debate issues such as, "If we
have captured maximum market share in our home market, let's
move on to other countries," or "Maybe the foreign market offers
even more profitable opportunities than our domestic market."

However, many transnational corporations may encounter problems if the destination country has established regulations about
who can or cannot do business in their jurisdiction, or even how
commerce can be transacted. A single corporation would probably

have little, if any, influence over relaxing or changing "do not enter" regulations. (A corporation such as Wal-Mart is likely the exception. It seems to be able to influence local governments to accept its presence even in the face of public opposition.) But a block of corporations or an industry group, acting through agents such as their national governments or trade commissions, has immense influence on political decisions. The tobacco, gun, and agricultural lobbies have all influenced the U.S. federal government to force open new markets or, conversely, erect trade barriers (including subsidies) to protect certain industries.

Thanks to such intervention and the agglomeration of political and corporate power, the boardroom discussion may include such questions as, "How do we influence this foreign government to amend their 'do not enter' legislation?"

EXPORTING INEQUITY:
THE GLOBAL ADVANCE OF CAPITALISM

The argument in favor of globalization is that when more trade routes and marketplaces are opened, the planet will know greater prosperity, peace, and ecological balance. This is the twentieth-century version of Adam Smith's capitalism with its "invisible hand." It was also one of the arguments Britain used when building its empire in the eighteenth century. In the preceding two centuries this view supported the economic justification for slavery.

From a free-enterprise point of view, this was an interesting argument twenty or thirty years ago when there was no apparent alternative to globalization. For example, what was inherently wrong with being able to purchase a bottle of Coca-Cola in India?

A generation later, and with global distances shrunk by technological and communications advances, this perspective has changed. In 2002, the Indian government sued both the Coca-Cola Company and PepsiCo Inc. for defacing Himalayan antiquities and natural beauty.

Both companies had painted their corporate logos on mountain rock faces and nailed signs to trees adjacent to the main highway in the Himachal Pradesh region of India. The transnational beverage conglomerates averaged four to five advertisements per kilometer on a fifty-six-kilometer stretch of road. Despite knowingly violating Indian law, they spent millions of dollars (costs eventually passed on to consumers) to present a legal defense. And, unfortunately, these are not isolated examples.

Governments in democratic countries are responsible to their citizens and have an obligation to look out for their best interests, but to whom are transnational corporations responsible? Stockholders are not elected, and, arguably, self-interest is their motivation. Globalization has meant that large and influential corporations, the inner workings of which we know surprisingly little about, now market their products and services in more countries than ever before.

In some countries where the conditions are favorable, transnationals have also opened up manufacturing plants. Again, on the surface, this appears to be a good idea, as it provides increased employment opportunities. However, more thorough examinations often reveal cases of child workers, poverty-level labor rates, non-existent health benefits, long working hours, and intolerable working conditions. On the other side of the coin is the reality that many jobs in the home country are sent overseas to enable these irresponsible practices.

In other words, a global company can advertise that it produces a world-class product for its various international markets, even while it does not adhere to the established labor, health, safety, and environmental standards of its home country. This country is usually a Western industrialized democracy, which has already signed treaties and conventions to support the International Labour Organization, as well as United Nations and European Union standards and requirements. In the face of such realities, executives often argue that meeting local standards and conditions is all that is required. Such a stance is ironic when one considers that one of the rationalizations behind globalization is to raise people's standard of living.

We find similar ironies when looking at the compensation packages for senior executives now working as expatriates. For example, a North American or European executive relocated to the position of president or managing director over a transnational's Bolivian operations would certainly not be paid in accordance with the pay-scale standards applied to Bolivian executives and certainly not in Bolivian currency. Strangely, it is acceptable to follow Bolivian compensation practices for employees but not for the senior management team—especially not for the expatriate president of a company.

Furthermore, every transnational corporation has a headquarters—a corporate boardroom—and it's unlikely that it is in the developing world. So where do citizen-groups in less developed nations go to argue for local jurisdiction over what is happening in their country? We have global markets where corporate decision-makers are difficult to access and countries where corporations have limited (if any) responsibility or accountability to indigenous cultures, communities, and environments. Legally, the primary responsibility of a corporation is not to a foreign country but to its stockholders; after all, they own the company.

THE CORPORATION, IN THE EYES OF THE BUDDHIST

The popular 2003 documentary film *The Corporation* (based on Joel Bakan's book) continued the shifting public understanding of the entity known as The Corporation. The book and the movie seek to explore this question: A corporation is treated with the same protections granted to people—but if it is a person, what kind of person is it? And the answer is unsettling: one who meets the diagnostic criteria for antisocial personality disorder—known more familiarly as a sociopath.

But let's look a little closer and try to define the corporation. It has a charter granted by a provincial/state or federal government agency. It has, in all likelihood, a building and an address, though these can be changed by executive decision. Likewise, staff can be hired, terminated, laid-off, relocated, or re-trained. In other words, *everything* about the corporation can be changed at the discretion of the executive team, with a simple amendment to the charter. (Of course, if the executive team does not constitute the majority of shareholders, then changing the charter also requires the approval of shareholders.)

One crucial point is that while corporations can amend their charters, the governments who granted them cannot revoke them. And while exceptional circumstances that would warrant the withdrawal of the charter, such as the not paying of taxes or not filing annual corporation documents, do exist, Enron, WorldCom, and Tyco all still have their charters. Despite what is essentially an

"What kind of tolerance does the Western culture call for, when this culture has convictions to the effect that dialogue and communications with other cultures should be to the benefit of the victorious culture, and thus, even values of positive globalization (democracy, human rights, etc.) are based on rejecting and excluding others?" —Mohamad Hussein

indefinite license to continue, we still cannot physically touch or hold on to a corporation. It is not a thing, though it is comprised of systems and processes that produce goods and services. And it is people who inform these processes. And, similar to all sentient beings, corporations must eat (take in raw materials), process the intake (manufacture products or services), eliminate waste, and replenish (work to sell these products for a profit). And, as Buddhist scholar Paul Harvey notes in the case of humans, "only partial control can be exercised over these processes; so they often change in undesirable ways, leading to suffering." The body becomes ill; the corporation becomes unhealthy.

There is a Buddhist concept that applies very well to the entity we call a corporation: *impermanence*. Buddhism holds that any object or idea comprised entirely of component parts without a self-existent and unchanging essence is always changing and thus needs to be understood as impermanent. A corporation— which is constructed from parts (people, departments, raw and finished materials, products and services, etc.)—fits these criteria and is therefore impermanent or in a state of constant change.

(The understanding of impermanence and the realization that an unchanging "self" does not exist—for I am just a manifestation of the changing world in which I live—is key to freedom from suffering.)

We can also make the argument that a person and a corporation are both subject to greed or excessiveness. For a person, the source of suffering is clinging to attachments—to have more, more of anything of which our "untrained mind" can conceive. For a corporation, the source of suffering is also an attachment to excess—in the form of anything the "untrained mind" can think of that will create more profit. In Buddhism, the "untrained mind" refers to a mind that has yet to understand that suffering can end when one lets go of attachment to excess, hatred, and the illusion that things are permanent. Neither the individual nor the corporation initially understands the source of attachments, the suffering they cause, and the way out of suffering. By not understanding the way out, the corporation continues to perpetuate suffering through the desire to expand, gain greater market share, and inevitably make more profit (incurring along the way all the problems that these processes involve).

REFORMING THE CORPORATION

With its mandate to maximize profit, the legal and impersonal being that is a corporate entity will continue to grow and do what its executives deem necessary to become a larger company or a global player. So the answer to the many problems of globalization does not lie with the corporation itself but with the customers, stockholders, and executives who currently believe that more profit is the only goal.

If *consumers* determined through their own inquiries, data gathering, and independent decisions that they did not wish to purchase products from Company A, then Company A would need to change. The U.S. tobacco companies have heard the message (at least in their home countries) and have diversified. When consumers stop purchasing items from Company A, Company A will need to rethink its business mission and strategies, otherwise it will lose customers and eventually go out of business.

Some suggestions for reforming the corporation include:

■ Require board members (directors and officers) to take responsibility to ensure that:

▶ all *social and environmental issues* are taken into consideration both before their company moves into a new jurisdiction and after it has established its operations;

▶ *open consultation* has taken place with communities prior to entering their market; and

▶ a greater degree of *disclosure*, transparency, and prior notice occurs before any major corporate business activity is to take place.

■ Extend the board's responsibility, and hence liability, to include personal responsibility for the corporation's compliance with the social and environmental laws of the countries in which the corporation does business.

■ Have transnational corporations become *accountable* legal entities in each country they do business in so that local investors and citizens have the right to take legal action in their home country.

If *stockholders,* who might also be customers, decide that they do not want their funds to support, for example, Company A's environmental record, they will sell their stock. When this happens enough times the value of the corporation on the stock market will diminish. Once that happens, the stockholders will have gained the attention of the senior executives and the board. It is then the executives' responsibility to determine why stock prices have fallen and make necessary corrections.

The *executive leadership team* also has an important role to perform in altering corporate direction. They can make changes by *living their conscience.* Even though executives may be immersed in an excessive materialist culture, change is always possible. Once people put their own integrity and the holistic well-being of themselves and all the communities to which they interdependently belong ahead of corporate interests, the corporation will change. Regaining personal integrity and finding wisdom will lead to business decisions that support the value of Causing No Harm.

These strategies are non-violent change from the inside. But we can also influence the direction of change from the outside. Before embarking, it is important to ask: "Do we want to change a specific corporation's direction or do we want to change the institution that we call The Corporation?" My view is that society cannot wait to reform corporations one at a time; too much damage to our culture and the environment will continue to take place as this process unfolds. It is wiser to reform the legal systems that give rise to corporations in the first place.

We can begin reforming the institution of The Corporation by requiring public reporting on environmental standards, labor practices in all facilities (foreign and domestic), community relations, etc., similar to the way publicly traded companies currently report their quarterly financial results. This reporting would focus on the damage already done as well as the future risks on both social issues (e.g., local communities, local industries, culture, etc.) and environmental issues (e.g., air and water pollution, clear-cut logging, chemical damage to the soil, etc.).

There are two reasons why public reporting is important: first, the process (and the public scrutiny that process would receive) would compel the board and executive team to focus on the issues that require reporting; and second, it creates a vehicle for the public, consumers, and investors to learn about the corporation's track record. Such information would fundamentally affect the way investors and customers make purchasing decisions.

OTHER ALTERNATIVES

The promise of access to opportunity has been hijacked by greed; the expected outcomes of traditional economic thinking have not materialized. In its present configuration, our materialistic society offers us little choice but to continue the human and environmental exploitation needed to survive in today's harsh world. These economic forces are damaging our society and destroying our environment.

For the last 250 years economists have done their best to be rational and create a science from which they can design models about how society can rise above its fears and its attachment to excess and subsequent environmental exploitation. From a Buddhist perspective more economic science, if done with the same premises, will not alter the current direction. We need to explore an approach that places human values, as a minimum, on the *same priority level as maximizing profits.*

To achieve this, a holistic or spiritual approach to life is needed. Not spirituality to the exclusion of economics or business, for the two can be mutually supportive of each other, but an approach that acknowledges that our humanity runs deep and appears in every aspect of our lives. To seek to live in balance with the way life and nature really are (that is, live the Middle Way) can bring us back to the benefits of community life and of having the economic locus of influence within the community. When people coalesce around the idea of community there is a strong drive to accept responsibility to acknowledge our care and connectedness with others.

COMMUNITIES THAT WORK: THE SLOW CITY

From a Buddhist perspective, community is a core component in living a holistic or spiritual life. The Buddhist description is of a community of individuals sharing their life's journey by striving for joy and happiness and the continual reduction of suffering.

While this may sound utopian, it is, in fact, happening. Let's look at two very different initiatives to Create a Better Society. Both operate within the free enterprise system but emphasize a greater balance between the need for human values and the need to be profitable.

The first is the Slow City Movement, which evolved from a Slow Food initiative started in Bra, Piedmont, Italy in 1986 as a local response to the fast food industry (especially McDonald's).

The international Slow Food Movement has grown from 20 member countries to more than 100, with more than 110,000 members organized in local chapters (including more than 90 in North America).

However, soon after the organization was started, it became

The Slow Food Movement asserts that the enjoyment of excellent food and drink should be combined with efforts to save the countless traditional grains, vegetables, fruits, animal breeds, and food products that are disappearing due to the prevalence of convenience food and industrial agribusiness. The movement points out that since 1900, 93% of American food product diversity has been lost and thirty thousand vegetable varieties have become extinct—and one more is lost every six hours. The movement organizes fairs, markets, and events locally and internationally to showcase products of excellent gastronomic quality and to offer discerning consumers the opportunity to meet producers.

Slow Food works to defend bio-diversity in our food supply, spread taste education, and connect producers of excellent foods with co-producers through events and initiatives.

The Slow Food Movement is also related to the Slow City Movement, which is growing quickly. In Germany, for example, the Slow City philosophy is being recognized increasingly as an alternative urban development vision and even larger cities are taking note of it in their efforts to do commercial revitalization. It is also important to note that Slow Cities could too easily be misinterpreted as regressive, isolationist, or backward communities. This is far from being true. Slow Cities want to be at the forefront of cutting-edge urban planning ideas, technology, and innovation. They are not against locating a McDonald's, but rather hope that through their efforts the citizens will become educated consumers who are aware of the local choices and options for getting fresh, healthful, and tasty meals. Slow Cities want to be eventful places where local traditions are celebrated and mixed with cosmopolitan influences. Unlike the slow-growth or no-growth movements in the U.S., Slow Cities are interested in growing, but to them what matters are the qualitative aspects of growth and development.

To become part of the Slow City Movement, a regional or city council must pass by-laws that include the following commitments (among others):

- To implement an *environmental* policy designed to maintain and develop the characteristics of the surrounding area and urban fabric, emphasizing recovery and reuse techniques.

- To implement an *infrastructure* policy that actively supports the improvement, not the occupation of the land.

- To promote the use of *technologies* that improve the quality of the environment.

- To safeguard local and home-grown/homemade production that is rooted in the region's *history, culture, and traditions;* and to promote preferential retail space for direct contact between customers, producers, and vendors.

- To promote the quality of *hospitality* as a real bond with the local community.

Eighty cities in Italy, Germany, Switzerland, England, Norway, Brazil, Japan, Greece, and Croatia are members of the Slow City Movement. At the time of publication there are no North American cities that have made the commitment.

clear that the Slow Food founders cared about issues much broader than the stress-producing twenty-minute lunch or non-nutritional meals, which they understood as signs of the deterioration of their lifestyle. From this broader concern was born the Slow City Movement. While clearly not Luddites, the movement's adherents are people who take the time to move thoughtfully, deliberately, and holistically through their lives.

The Slow City Movement is now active in Italy, as well as in eight other European, Asian, and North American countries. This local initiative grew in response to many of the negative aspects of globalization: a sameness in mass-produced goods, the extensive use of non-renewable resources, the sacrificing of quality in the pursuit of lower prices, the obstruction of natural beauty by advertising and marketing signage, etc.

To articulate their philosophy, the Movement's first president, Carl Petrini, cited a little-known seventeenth-century Italian writer, Francesco Angelita, who once devoted an entire book to snails. Angelita privileged slowness as an essential virtue, and praised snails' adaptability and ability to settle anywhere.

Since its founding, the Slow City Movement has seen over sixty cities worldwide sign a civic charter requiring them to create a balance between the modern and the traditional, thereby promoting a good quality of life. If we look for similarities between the intentions of the Slow City Movement and the Buddha's teachings we find a unique twenty-first century European application of the Middle Way.

COMMUNITIES THAT WORK: SARVODAYA

A second holistic community initiative is one that, for the present, operates only in Sri Lanka. The founder, Dr. Ari. T. Ariyaratne, gave the Sanskrit word *Sarvodaya,* meaning "the awakening of all," as both the name and mission of the movement. The philosophy of the Sarvodaya Movement is rooted in both the Buddha's teachings as well Mahatma Gandhi's non-violent approaches to community and nation building. Dr. Ariyaratne has described the intention behind the movement this way: "The goal of the Sarvodaya Movement is to liberate the goodness that is inherent in every person."

Dr. Ariyarante, in his acceptance speech for the 1996 Gandhi Peace Prize (awarded by the government of India), observed that "a global transformation of human consciousness is needed to bring humanity closer to peace and justice." He believes that our current political and economic systems inevitably result in the poor becoming poorer. While developing Buddhist-based methods for addressing the problem of poverty, he is solidly committed to achieving this transformation non-violently.

The Sarvodaya Movement, for almost fifty years, has been supporting such transformation in the rural communities of Sri Lanka. From its early beginnings in one village, it has grown to encompass over fifteen thousand villages throughout the island—including Buddhist, Hindu, and Christian communities.

During this time, Sri Lanka has been riddled with poverty and divided by political and religious strife. Sri Lanka, like many other Asian counties, has been caught up in the globalized economy and is home to many branch factories of electronics and textiles. As we have seen elsewhere—even in North America—the poor gain some benefits from such industrialization, but the poverty/affluence gap continues to widen. Economic growth has not eradicated this problem; in many cases, it has exacerbated it.

Although in Sri Lanka exports have been increasing and overall income has risen, economic wealth has not reached the population evenly. While the island's cities and corporations have experienced growth, the quality of life in rural areas has not improved. In the agricultural sector, many Sri Lankans continue to live at or below the poverty level. Industrialization has also created a new urban underclass whose earnings have increased but who still cannot afford to feed themselves.

The results of this unbalanced development can be seen in the country's rates of suicide, violent crime, and alcoholism. Left out of the growing prosperity they see elsewhere in the country, many people feel powerless to help themselves. In many cases, they have become desperate and self-destructive.

These are communities that are *suffering*. To turn these circumstances around, Dr. Ariyarante proposed a Buddhist solution, where the ultimate goal is happiness and the awakening of our true nature.

THE SARVODAYA APPROACH

The Sarvodaya organization evolved the following five-stage self- and community-development program to actualize its goals:

Stage 1. People from a selected village and Sarvodaya volunteers from neighboring villages participate in planning sessions and then develop essential services such as roads, wells, agricultural irrigation, reforestation programs, etc., with the emphasis on realizing the greatest benefit for all members of the community.

Stage 2. Peer groups from within the village population (e.g., mothers' groups, youth groups, etc.) are formed. These groups are given training in leadership and decision-making skills so that they can effectively participate, along with the volunteers, in providing the ten basic needs (see box on page 79).

Stage 3. Through self-reliance and community participation the basic needs in the village are satisfied and a village-level Sarvodaya Society is formed to give organized leadership to all

"My story is not so much in what Sarvodaya, as an organization, does to start, nurture, and support businesses. It is the overall philosophy that says we need to create and nurture what I would call a psychosocial and spiritual 'infrastructure' as a basis for economic development and business strategies. I have always said—and Sarvodaya's philosophy and practice have demonstrated—that if we focus on earning money and 'doing business' before establishing the values orientation which encompasses kindness, compassionate action, altruistic joy, and equanimity, we will find that people get into conflict over money. To be frank, the sharing that makes the difference is the giving; not the 'I want my share.'

"Does this approach set us up to resent wealth? No, it should not, because if we are sufficiently detached from material and transitory things we don't overly concern ourselves with getting, keeping, and protecting what we have. Sometimes the notion of a society with neither poverty nor affluence seems unreasonable to those whose lives have become comfortable at the higher end of the socioeconomic scale. Especially to entrepreneurs who cherish the opportunities to be challenged and feel so rewarded by the monetary profits that accrue to 'success.' Not aiming to be a millionaire can seem demotivating. But the emergence of the entire field of social entrepreneurship addresses such seeming conflicts of values. Simply put, there is a lot more to business success than what we know as monetary profit."

—Dr. A.T. Ariyaratne

> **THE SARVODAYA MOVEMENT'S "TEN BASIC HUMAN NEEDS FOR ALL INDIVIDUALS IN A JUST SOCIETY"**
>
> - A clean and beautiful environment
> - A clean and adequate supply of water
> - Basic clothing
> - A balanced diet
> - A simple house to live in
> - Basic health care
> - Simple communication facilities
> - Basic energy requirements
> - Well-rounded education
> - Cultural and spiritual sustenance

village-level activities that lead to the improvement of living standards.

Stage 4. Economic development activities are introduced to the village, progressively developing the capacity of the people to save, borrow, improve existing enterprises, start new ones, repay loans, and finally to evolve their own village development bank.

Stage 5. Economic relationships with neighboring villages are built, strengthening their capacity to share wealth, products, and services so that development takes place in a cluster of villages. The clusters of villages throughout the country contribute to the building of an alternative approach to economic development, which benefits rural areas.

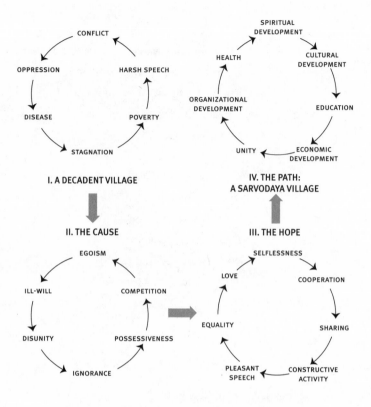

FIGURE 5.1: SARVODAYA—A VILLAGE AWAKENING

PERMISSION GRANTED BY DR. A.T. ARIYARATNE, FOUNDER SARVODAYA
SHRAMADANA MOVEMENT. ADAPTED FROM SARVODAYA CHARTS.

THINK LOCAL, ACT GLOBAL

Economic growth is essential. However, to be in keeping with
the goals of skillful action and skillful intention, it has to respect
the rights of all life on the planet, promote equal and non-
exploitative relationships among human beings, and recognize
the interdependence between human beings, society, and nature.
The two initiatives described above—one European and one

Asian—are creative examples in which communities have come together to facilitate what today we would call sustainable development. In both cases, a greater balance between human values and unrestricted capitalism has been brought to bear on the free enterprise system. In the case of the Sarvodaya Movement, some people will become entrepreneurs, creating employment and prosperity, while still adhering to the value of Causing No Harm.

To influence the future direction of capitalism, we need to grow and support more examples in which communities have said "No" to unrestricted free enterprise and its effects. An economy that acknowledges our societal and environmental connections as core principles can advance capitalism. Such an economy will acknowledge that assisting others is the prerequisite for ensuring the well-being of ourselves and of those we are dependent upon. Transforming the global economy in accordance with spiritual and ethical values must become each individual's unique responsibility at this critical time in our economic history.

By walking away from greed, the global economy has the opportunity to reinvent itself. By following the Middle Way, we avoid the extremes of poverty and extravagance, and naturally acknowledge our most compassionate values.

SECTION 3: PROGNOSIS

THE MIDDLE WAY TO A HEALTHY ORGANIZATION

> "Because we know a path out of suffering,
> our way of acting in the world as Buddhists
> and applying social justice is to teach others ...
> so that they themselves can use these tools
> and become free."
>
> JAN CHOZEN BAYS

6

BUDDHIST BUILDING BLOCKS:
DHARMA, KARMA,
AND THE FOUR NOBLE TRUTHS

TWENTY-FIVE hundred years ago, near the border with present-day Nepal, Siddhartha Gautama was born into a royal family in northeastern India. Despite his family's wealth and status, he was moved by the suffering he saw all around him: illness, disease, poverty, drudgery, malaise, and death. He could find no satisfying explanation for the pain people experienced, or were likely to experience, in their lives. So he made it his life's mission to get to the bottom of this.

Initially, Siddhartha followed the custom of the day and joined a small group of like-minded seekers, ascetics, who believed that the answer lay in personal deprivation. After six years of suffering and nearly starving to death, Siddhartha realized this approach was not going to provide him the answer he sought. On the other hand, the opulence of his parents' palaces, where all his needs (except, notably, the spiritual ones) were met, had not provided the answer, either.

After regaining his health, Siddhartha chose another method for uncovering the truth about suffering: he sat beneath a bodhi tree and turned his mind unwaveringly on the questions of how suffering arose and how it could be made to pass away. In other words, he meditated. After the deepest reflection and observation, he had the answer to his question. Siddhartha Gautama has come to be known to us, of course, as the Buddha. The answer Siddhartha found is set out in his first teaching, referred to as the Setting in Motion of the Dharma-Wheel.

In this chapter, we will look at the Four Noble Truths that make up the Setting in Motion of the Dharma-Wheel and will begin to explore the implications that these have for our business practices. But before we get there, an understanding of some other fundamental Buddhist beliefs is important.

THE BUDDHIST'S TOOLKIT

One could relive the experiences of Siddhartha, follow his journey through various extremes, and devote time to intensive meditation, and come to the same findings and conclusions as he did. Since most people would not want to go to these lengths, the Buddha taught about his experiences, which are a methodology or "Path" to follow in overcoming suffering and attaining Enlightenment. This Path constitutes a wealth of understanding. At the heart of the Path we find the Four Noble Truths and the Law of Cause and Effect: two core teachings that constitute the substance of the Middle Way, the Path between extremes that is the focus of Buddhism as discussed in this book.

Buddhism is first and foremost an *empirical method* to progressively work toward the well-being of oneself and others. Calling

Buddhism empirical may surprise some. Buddhism is not a religion in our Judeo-Christian sense; it offers us a new way of addressing the ills of our society. Not grounded in dogmatic theology, the "mysteries" revealed by the Buddha were discovered in a fashion consistent with the Western empirical method: hypothesis, observation, examination, and conclusion.

For each of us, the Buddhist journey starts with an acknowledgment that all individuals experience suffering as a result of not letting go—not detaching from our desires or cravings—and not appreciating the reality of impermanence. Buddhists say we are living in *samsara*—in a cycle of suffering that includes a succession of births and rebirths, which continue until we have attained liberation from our attachments and, finally, Nirvana. Nirvana is a state of existence that is free from desire, hatred, delusions, and the determining effects of karma (our intentional action and their consequences). In a sense, Nirvana is success in the fullest, for as the Buddha said: "One may defeat a thousand obstacles and adversaries, yet he who defeats the enemies within is the noblest victor."

The word *Dharma,* which refers to the teachings of the Buddha, also has a second meaning. It is, in a sense, a Buddhist term that describes the universal order of things. Scholar Damien Keown describes the Dharma as "a universal law, which governs both the physical and moral order of the universe."

Though increasingly common in popular culture (and therefore increasingly misunderstood), the word *karma* is the Sanskrit word for "action." Buddhists, however, are more specific in their use of the word, and use it to refer to actions related to moral choices and the consequences of such behavior. Our choices in such situations—indeed, our *intentions*—are instrumental in shaping, in Keown's words, "our natures for good or ill."

All our actions in life are a result of what we think, what we do, and what we say. Karma is embedded within each of these actions. Any action that is driven by the intentions of love, compassion, and/or wisdom carries with it wholesome karma or joy. Conversely, any thought or deed done with malicious intentions is unwholesome karma and adds negative tendencies to the outcome. Unwholesome karmic energy will have a negative consequence.

The Buddha's argument was that the desire to eliminate all unhappiness (suffering) can only be realized if the causes of unhappiness are known and removed. Eliminate the causes of suffering and the unhappiness will stop. By knowing and understanding these causes, we will then know what actions to take.

APPLYING THE FOUR NOBLE TRUTHS

Let's have a look at how the Sarvodaya Movement has adapted the Buddha's teaching to an economic problem. They saw in a village that people are suffering in poverty and hopelessness, and they saw how this begot more suffering (this is the First Noble Truth). They saw the Second Noble Truth in the way individual greed and distrust (competition for existing limited resources) eroded an individual's and the community's intentions and energies. And they saw the Third Noble Truth in the fact that people have the inherent potential to create a caring community (it is a matter of intention, of choice, not fate). And finally, they actualized the Fourth Noble truth in applying their guiding principles to help people make choices and decisions that create self-reliant, caring, and productive individuals and communities.

This summary is a simplification of the amazingly transformative work that Sarvodaya has enabled. By providing a way to understand not only a community's failings but also its way out of suffering, Sarvodaya has helped over fifteen thousand Sri Lankan villagers to become self-sufficient.

It should be noted that the power of the Four Noble Truths is diminished if you consider any of them in isolation. Perhaps, therefore, the best representation of the work of Sarvodaya is not a series of bullet points discussing each Noble Truth but a single diagram that illustrates this process and the interconnectedness of each of the Four Noble Truths (Figure 5.1).

MOVING FORWARD ON THE PATH

The Sarvodaya model may work most easily for not-for-profit organizations because their initial intentions frequently contain human values and not just the profit motive. But, as we discuss and rethink the priorities of businesses and organizations, we will expand on Dr. Ariyaratne's model and apply it to commercial enterprises. In the meantime, the Four Noble Truths are such a critical point in Buddhist thought that it's worth looking at them,

> Unlike the philosophies of Greece and of the early religious leaders, Buddhism has never given much importance to questions such as, "Where did we come from?" and "Who created the universe?" Buddhism focuses more on seeing reality clearly for what it is, and thereby ending the cycles of suffering, than on debating cosmology and metaphysics.

again, this time, from a somewhat different perspective. If we view the Buddha's teachings as those of a wise and compassionate family doctor, we can see the Four Noble Truths as his methodology:

▶ Symptom: Suffering

▶ Diagnosis: Attachment, craving, desiring

▶ Prognosis: Liberation from attachment is possible

▶ Prescription: The Noble Eightfold Path/Eight
   Guiding Principles

Using this simplified medical analogy enables us to assess where we've come and to signpost where we are going. The first sections of this book (Chapters 1–5) highlighted the nature of suffering, not only the obvious, telegenic suffering that generates media coverage and benefit concerts but also the suffering that free enterprise engenders in all strata of the developing world. This enabled us to identify the ways in which our attachments (the Three Poisons) perpetuate our suffering.

The next section (Chapters 6–10) of this book—the Buddhist principles—examines the ways out of suffering. The prognosis I will suggest is grounded in the Buddhist notion that liberation from our attachments is possible. This Buddhist framework will continue with a more detailed look at the Noble Eightfold Path, as well as economic and ethical business practices. The final section of the book (Chapters 11–12) will make some initial suggestions about a prescription for free enterprise.

"The question is not whether an individual is rich or poor but whether he is good or bad, virtuous or sinful. It is actions that qualitatively determine the greatness of a person."

DR. ARI T. ARIYARATNE

7

EIGHT IS ENOUGH:
THE GUIDING PRINCIPLES OF THE
NOBLE EIGHTFOLD PATH

IN THIS CHAPTER we will explore the Fourth Noble Truth—the prescription, or the way out of suffering—the Noble Eightfold Path. We will examine the ways in which each step on the Path is not only a move toward ending individual suffering but can also contribute to building healthy organizations that Cause No Harm.

The Noble Eightfold Path can be divided into three groups of what I will call Guiding Principles. Each Guiding Principle and group of Guiding Principles brings with it the intention of developing within the individual sufficient skills to successfully detach from those mental states (desiring, craving, aversion) that cause dissatisfaction, pain, and suffering.

Guiding Principles 1 and 2

Wisdom: clearly understanding the causes of and means to eliminate pain and suffering.

| Guiding Principles 3 to 5 | *Ethical conduct*: virtuous intentions and behaviors toward yourself, others, and nature. |
| Guiding Principles 6 to 8 | *Compassion*: cultivating a good heart and mind. |

WISDOM

Guiding Principle 1: Skillful Understanding

The goal of Skillful Understanding is to provide a perspective for interpreting the holistic nature of life as described by the Fourth Noble Truth. This first step on the Path allows us to examine and then understand our beginning point, our destination, and the milestones in between.

We begin with an interpretation of ourselves, others, and our organizations. An understanding of who we truly are leads us to observe the actions we undertake. This understanding is the foundation of the choices we make and the goals we establish, and directly affects the way we implement these goals. For example, a highly competitive and driven corporate leader who sees the world as "there for the taking" would likely want to possess far in excess of need (greed), want to increase market share and put competitors out of business (hatred), and take actions based on the illusion of permanence and self-existence (ignorance). We can easily see these behaviors in others; Skillful Understanding is about seeing our own intentions and actions.

Skillful Understanding requires a comprehensive appreciation of the ethics of our intentions, our thoughts, and our subsequent actions—what we labelled as karma in Chapter 6. To understand karma is to understand one of the essential messages of this book.

Long before I undertook the study of Buddhism, I was aware that what I did had consequences. Doing good things seemed to make other good things happen. My awareness of this probably came from my father, who used to counsel, "Whenever you decide to do something, think it through, because in the end you are responsible for the results."

Learning about karma helped me piece together the puzzle. Karma is the result of our actions—not just accidental actions, but actions that are thought out or deliberate. And it is this deliberateness (or intentionality) that defines one's moral and ethical values. From a Buddhist perspective, skillful behavior is based on the Law of Cause and Effect. If during the annual auditor's meeting, for example, we decide to withhold the whole truth and only provide what is asked for, what is the karmic value of this action? An answer that represents deliberate deception will, at some point, have negative consequences. If the motive or intention underlying an action is based in causing harm, the resulting consequence will be unwholesome. As Bhikkhu Bodhi notes: "The most important feature about karma is its capacity to produce results corresponding to the ethical quality of the action."

Refraining from unskillful behavior, in thought, intention, or action is not a commandment from on high. To refrain, in the Buddhist perspective, is a conscious and voluntary action of the individual, which is grounded in an understanding of the Four Noble Truths. To refrain is to have the wisdom to apply an ethical code within all aspects of our life. This is the essence of Skillful Understanding. Not only *can* the individual effect change—significant societal change at that—but change *must* be the result of individual intentions, informed by an appreciation of karma.

Guiding Principle 2: Skillful Thought

The core of this Guiding Principle is the focus or intention of our thoughts. The second step in the Buddha's Path is intended to help us better understand the scope of healthy thought processes and move us toward a correct understanding of reality and karma. To achieve this, the Buddha described Skillful Thought as comprising three components. Considered together, these lead to positive karma and positive outcomes. They support the development of wisdom and strengthen our intention to Cause No Harm. The three components of Skillful Thought are Repudiating Desire, Intending Goodwill, and Intending Harmlessness:

> ▶ *Repudiating Desire.* It is only in repudiating our desires that we can achieve freedom from desire—true happiness. By changing our perception about having more to a belief in fewer attachments, we deny the emergence of those cravings that lead to suffering.

As Bhante Henepola Gunaratana encourages in *Eight Mindful Steps to Happiness:* "What we need to reject is not the things we have, or our family and friends, but rather our mistaken sense that these people are our possessions. We need to let go of our habit of clinging to the people and the material things in our lives and to our ideas, beliefs, and opinions."

> ▶ *Intending Goodwill.* Goodwill is a characteristic of Skillful Thought because it counteracts unwholesome or negative thoughts such as anger and aversion; or anxiety, depression, and possibly violence. Counteracting thoughts and intentions grounded in wishing ill-will or harm to others generates deeply rooted loving-kindness.

The nature of this love is not necessarily what we experience when loving our children, spouse, or extended family; it is a form of love that affects our relationship to ourselves and all other

Bhante Henepola Gunaratana's *Eight Mindful Steps to Happiness* offers some practical steps for overcoming the anger that often stands in the way of harmlessness. Consider these reminders, adapted from the teachings of Bhante Gunaratana, as you begin your journey to wisdom:

- Become aware of your anger as soon as possible;
- Be mindful of your anger and feel its strength;
- Remember that a quick temper is extremely dangerous;
- Bring to mind anger's miserable consequences;
- Practice restraint;
- Change your attitude by becoming helpful and kind;
- Change the atmosphere between you and a person with whom you are angry by offering a gift or a favor;
- Remember the advantages of practicing loving-kindness;
- Remember we all will die one day, and we don't want to die with anger.

beings. Loving-kindness (*metta*) is cultivated through meditation that transforms our thoughts and intentions from creating harm for others to compassion. And, in the words of Bhikkhu Bodhi, "through practice the feeling of love becomes ingrained, grafted onto the mind as a natural and spontaneous tendency."

Intending goodwill and cultivating loving-kindness are not far removed from Gandhi's beliefs about non-violence. "If we are to be non-violent," the Mahatma wrote, "we must then not wish for anything on this earth which the meanest or the lowest of human beings cannot have."

> ▶ *Intending Harmlessness.* This intention is expressed suc-
> cinctly by Bhikkhu Bodhi: "The intention of harmlessness is
> thought guided by compassion, aroused in opposition to
> cruel, aggressive, and violent thoughts."

Focusing mental discipline on these three things (repudiating desire, intending goodwill, and intending harmlessness) will eliminate negative intentions.

And the source of our karma lies with our intentions.

ETHICAL CONDUCT

Guiding Principle 3: Skillful Speech

The key to Skillful Speech is an appreciation that the words that come out of our mouths—be they ideas, suggestions, complaints, disciplinary actions, praise, whatever—originate in our minds.

In the *Dhammapada,* Buddha cautions: "Let one be watchful of speech-irritation. Let him practice restraint of speech. Having abandoned the sins of speech, let him practice virtue with his speech." To be skillful, we need to understand and resist (as an act of self-discipline) the impulse to lie, swear, threaten, gossip, or verbally dominate—behaviors that all too often arise in meetings and boardrooms. If we knowingly stop unskillful speech, individually and then as groups, we will inevitably engage in speech that is truthful, considerate, and beneficial to the listener—and the marketplace.

In this way, we will begin to promote harmony, rather than more suffering. And, in the promotion of harmony, the ultimate outcome of Skillful Speech is manifesting wisdom. Bhikkhu Bodhi advises that "to realize truth our whole being has to be brought into accord with actuality, with things as they are, which requires that in communications with others we respect things as they are by speaking the truth."

> The Guiding Principle of Skillful Speech is valuable in promoting a positive workplace environment if we remember these four key points:
>
> - *Always be truthful in what you say.* What we say or write always comes from our thoughts and intentions.
>
> - *Do not use words to hurt others.* If your goal is to manipulate colleagues, team members, or customers by starting false rumors about a person or event then your speech is not grounded in positive or constructive intentions; it is not skillful and will lead to negative actions, which, like all actions, make up one's karma.
>
> - *Do not engage in profanity, verbal abuse, or harmful criticism.* The opposite of harsh or harmful speech is to train oneself in tolerance, and to respect different perspectives without becoming emotionally or personally engaged with criticism.
>
> - *Avoid meaningless talk such as gossip.* Gossip is frequently the cause of rumors, and rumors can sideline or even destroy well-intended people and plans.

As business leaders, the more we focus on "we win, you lose," the more we are thinking unskillfully, which leads inevitably to unskillful speaking. The actual duration or timeline of winning or losing is fleeting, it exists moment-by-moment and will never occur again. Compassion has a much longer karmic life.

When, as business people, we talk about gaining market share at the expense of putting another company out of business, or about convincing the public that a small or insignificant change in our product is a big customer benefit, we are engaged in unskillful speech. Does changing the shape of a beverage bottle contribute to a better society? Does it even contribute to a better-tasting beverage?

A positive workplace environment depends on what we communicate to each other.

Positive intentions concerning speech include truthfulness, not engaging in verbal harm or abuse, and the avoidance of profanity and meaningless talk.

Guiding Principle 4: Skillful Actions

As a Guiding Principle in business, Skillful Actions should be relatively easy to follow. The focus is on the outcomes of our actions. Harmful or unskillful actions are the result of hurtful (or unskillful) thoughts—this is one example of the interconnectedness of the Noble Eightfold Path.

Unskillful actions are to some extent included as offenses in our legal system, so every business leader should see him- or herself playing by the same rules. These behaviors only occur when our not-so-focused mind is overcome with anger, greed, and delusion about what is reality.

The larger point, however, is that Skillful Actions cannot be measured solely on the basis of existing legislation. The legal system has an uneasy relationship with morality and ethics, and when it does enter that realm, we have lengthy and protracted debates and very little clear definition. What is lawful may not be ethically correct or morally sound, given the definitions and context.

Skillful Action requires us to see beyond what is lawful into what is skillful (i.e., Causing No Harm) and unskillful (causing suffering). Like all moral and ethical decisions, we have to question our own intentions. Actions taken on the grounds of hatred, greed, or delusion will never be ethical.

If a particular law in a corporation's home country, for example, is more all-encompassing (more ethical) than a similar law in another country where the company does business, the law offering higher standards should apply. So, Skillful Action requires all investors, executives, and management committees to look at their individual thoughts, words, and subsequent actions in light of the suffering that they do or do not cause.

The tobacco and liquor industries would be hard pressed, in my opinion, to argue in favor of the non-suffering lifestyle or life-long benefits of their products. Additionally, executives and organizations that operate beyond the rules should be culpable and liable to be prosecuted for their actions or omissions (as were executives at Enron, Tyco, Hollinger, and WorldCom). On the other hand, an organic farmer who grows safe and nutritious food and a contractor who makes adequate use of solar, geothermal, or wind power to generate non-polluting energy would have little difficulty making an ethical case for the non-suffering caused by their products.

Guiding Principle 5: Skillful Livelihood

Skillful Livelihood means earning one's living in lawful, ethical, and moral ways. This Guiding Principle requires that one's livelihood not create suffering or harm for oneself or for others, and that it not be in violation of the other seven Guiding Principles.

Employment in industries that cause harm or death would be outside this Guiding Principle. Hence employment in the military or armament industries, whose sole purpose is to create weapons that kill or injure others, is in direct violation of this principle. Livelihoods through stealing, fraud, bribery, or gambling also cause harm, create negative karmic consequences, and have the potential for engendering revenge. Selling poisonous chemicals, intoxicants, or bodies (e.g., slavery or prostitution) are also obvious instances of unskillful livelihoods.

You can thoughtfully inquire into your own job or career. If what you do, or if what your organization does, violates the Five Precepts, the work you and your employer are involved in is unskillful livelihood. Your work would be defined, in Buddhist terms, as unethical. Remember, though, that any organization over time can see its ethical intentions change for the better or the worse. Our object in practicing Skillful Livelihood is to participate in an organization or work that positively inclines our mind toward peacefulness, compassion, and wisdom.

COMPASSION

Guiding Principle 6: Skillful Effort

Beginning to make Skillful Effort requires a slowing down, so that we can divest ourselves of negative states of mind. Business people accustomed to spending their work lives "putting out fires" may find this a challenge. Especially since high-energy behavior that thrives on excitement and immediate gratification has for many leaders become an attachment.

SKILLFUL (POSITIVE) EFFORT	UNSKILLFUL (NEGATIVE) THOUGHT/ACTION
Rational and clear thinking; not disproportionately concerned with "I" or "me."	Subjective, irrational thinking; ideas generated in the heat of passion.
Seeing the big picture, knowing the Middle Path, and not becoming entangled and losing one's objectivity.	Our mind and our thoughts becoming entangled so that we cannot see the difference between the two.
Knowing how our attachments lead to suffering.	Continually increasing attachments to greed, hatred, and illusions.
Wanting and needing little; not greedy.	Wanting too much, too many objects, and too much consumerism.
Being content with our thoughts, our person, and our surroundings.	Having a lowered level of self-respect; never being satisfied.
Being at peace with ourselves, appreciating the value of solitude, quiet time, and meditation.	Not being comfortable with ourselves, unable to achieve tranquillity, and using unskillful speech to camouflage our discomfort.
Applying discipline and concentration to our thoughts and behavior; expending effort to be in control of our mind and its positive thoughts.	Not expending the energy to control our thoughts; not weeding out the mind's laziness; being mentally restless, daydreaming.
Being positive and self-sufficient, generally not needing to rely upon others.	Being insecure about oneself and requiring others to listen to your travails and provide mental and emotional support.

Skillful Effort can help us to overcome everyday preoccupa-
tions, whether in our personal life or our business interactions.

To achieve the mental focus and discipline needed to overcome
the Five Hindrances (see glossary), the Buddha provided us with
three instructional steps to better understand the working of our
mind. The Guiding Principle of Skillful Effort teaches us to:

1. Prevent negative states of mind;

2. Overcome negative states of mind once they've arisen; and

3. Maintain and cultivate positive states of mind.

The chart on page 101 suggests some examples of the thoughts
that result from Skillful Efforts and their opposite—negative or
unskillful thoughts.

Skillful Effort requires the patience and the discipline to initially slow down, so that our minds too can slow down. Once
calmed, we can focus on our thoughts and intentions.

Guiding Principle 7: Skillful Mindfulness

To be mindful is to understand how to use our mind. This Guiding Principle, like all the other steps on the Buddha's Path, is a
personal self-development program—we can think of it as learning a new life skill.

The learning objective is to see to the core of ourselves by
detaching our minds from bias and opinions, concepts and constructs, and interpretations of perception. By learning to do this,
our mind becomes sharp, undistorted, and able to penetrate
deeply. The main tool for developing this skill is meditation.
(Meditation and its application are so to central to cultivating the
perspective espoused in this book that an introduction to meditation is included as Appendix III.)

Without any training, the mind normally flits from one thought to another. Meditators call this phenomenon "monkey mind" after the action of playful monkeys quickly jumping from one branch to another. This is quite normal for us, given the pace of today's business community. From a Buddhist perspective, however, such an environment produces ill-informed management decisions, brought about by unskillful mindfulness. The goal is to actually perform all activities mindfully—speaking, problem solving, breathing, eating, etc.—and to gain mental clarity about these activities. It is through the practice of meditation and the calmness and insight it brings to our mind that one sees one's world as it truly is.

This is where the Buddhist idea of living-in-the-moment comes from. Being present moment-by-moment is not what most of us are naturally inclined to do. For the most part we are certainly not trained to do it. Being here, right now, means to be aware of the physical and mental movements we make every minute of every day.

Being mindful is to see each moment as a separate event, so that we can be aware of the uniqueness of each moment without the attachments of what Bhante Gunaratana calls "socially conditioned responses or habitual reactions." Through Skillful Mindfulness we see our anxieties for what they really are: a simple experience of fear. We realize that this fear is not *us*, but is simply a mental phenomenon, a reflection of our attachment to previous experiences or perceptions, or to future outcomes. We are not our fears, our biases, our perceptions, or our beliefs or thoughts—these are all mere constructions that our mind has accepted over our lifetime. Through this self-development program of seeing who we are *now*—and then in the next moment and in the next—each moment is seen by an uncluttered mind as different from the previous moment and the one that follows.

In Buddhist fashion we learn first to see ourselves clearly (to the core of our being) and from these personal observations, we learn to see clearly into other issues, concerns, problems, and opportunities in the external world.

Guiding Principle 8: Skillful Concentration

This Guiding Principle, like the previous one, is meditation-based. We can realize the importance the Buddha placed on meditation and the need to use our minds skillfully by noting that two of the Eight Steps on his Path are based on understanding the nature of our thoughts, our intentions, and our actions, so as to ensure that we make wise choices and decisions.

As Bhante Gunaratana summarizes:

> Generally, when we say that someone is "concentrating" we can mean anything from being engrossed in a television show to strategizing in a chess game to plotting a crime. But the "concentration" the Buddha taught as part of his Noble Eightfold Path has three special characteristics: it is always wholesome; it goes into very deep and powerful levels of one-pointed focus; and it incorporates the use of mindfulness to develop wisdom.

Clearly, this type of "concentration" is more common to Buddhism than to boardrooms. But that does not mean that it cannot offer benefits to both.

PRINCIPLES AND VALUES

The Guiding Principles of the Noble Eightfold Path are not company-specific. They do not begin with the organization—they

> "Time pressures are often linked to the need to work long hours to support consumption habits—and to upgrade, store, or otherwise maintain possessions. Americans are among the most overworked people in the industrial world, putting in 350 hours (9 work weeks) more on the job each year than the average European."
> —Worldwatch Institute

start with you and me. The Guiding Principles can be a useful compass for our intentions, but will likely require that we think outside the boundaries of traditional economic thought. If we hold tight to *unrestricted* free enterprise, then human values and the environment will always be in competition with the big prize—profit.

The Guiding Principles are not commandments. They represent a rational and defensible plan to improve the quality of human life. If we, as leaders, acknowledge the Guiding Principles as a personal code of thought, intention, and action, then acceptance by our organization is a natural next step. Harmony between personal and corporate values is essential if organizations are going to live the values they proclaim. The challenge is to integrate the Guiding Principles with existing management practices and to demonstrate how a corporation can include Guiding Principles in their organizational processes. What might that look like?

Not only are the Guiding Principles useful as a set of ideals upon which an organization can base its Values, they can also be a helpful tool in explaining these Values in terms that all members of the organization can understand and follow. Furthermore, they can help define the actions that can make the Values come alive within the organization, and can provide a clarity of communication that ensures a common understanding among all stakeholders.

Let's look at a possible model for a Values Statement consistent with the principle of Causing No Harm, based on our initial sketch from Chapter 2, and parse it in the context of the Eight Guiding Principles.

CAUSE NO HARM VALUES STATEMENT

[a] A core value of our company is to be continuously mindful of our intentions and to contribute positively to the making of "better communities" among our internal and external stakeholders.

[b] We work and conduct business in a spirit of partnership.

[c] All interactions between people, as well as our environment, are based in a solid belief in respect and decency.

[d] We are committed to self-knowledge and development.

[e] We respect all individual differences.

[f] We appreciate that change is inevitable.

[g] We have a passion for our products and services.

[h] We will not acquire any raw materials, or design, manufacture, or sell any products or services, the doing of which will be harmful to beings or the environment.

Taking a holistic view, the principle of Causing No Harm (embodied in all of these statements) illustrates an organization's intention to be an outstanding corporate citizen. That is, its intention is to Cause No Harm and to proactively contribute to building a better society among all stakeholders, arguably the best exemplar for the current Corporate Social Responsibility initiatives.

Statements *b* through *e* specifically addresses Human Resource Values that progressive and socially responsible corporations can establish. The words might vary from one organization to the next, but the Values remain similar.

The first Guiding Principle—Skillful Understanding—tells us that the intentions and actions related to a "spirit of partnership" (statement *b*) are to be constructive, supportive, and not harmful. The second Guiding Principle—Skillful Thought—would have us look into our own hearts and minds to validate that our intentions are based on a desire for partnership and not, for example, on manipulation.

The Guiding Principle of Mindfulness would have us look patiently and insightfully into ourselves so that our passions are seen in a clear light. This requires recognition that goodness, like

> An introduction to meditation is provided in Appendix III. There are many other excellent introductions to meditation available, and I strongly recommend you explore one or more of them. Among the best of them are the following:
>
> *Mindfulness in Plain English,* by Bhante Henepola Gunaratana
>
> *Breath by Breath,* by Larry Rosenberg
>
> *Zen Meditation in Plain English,* by John Daishin Buksbazen
>
> *Insight Meditation,* by Joseph Goldstein

all other characteristics, is impermanent and hence must be given moment-to-moment attention (statement f).

Similarly, "a passion for our products and services" (statement g) illustrates the Guiding Principle of Skillful Livelihood. This is meant to ensure that all products and services will contribute positively to the well-being of others.

The same Guiding Principles that form the Path that Buddhists follow in working toward ending suffering can be used to build an organization that follows the principle of Causing No Harm, and subsequently to Creating a Better Society. It is also the same Path that provides the framework to modify unrestricted free enterprise so that profit-making and the well-being of society are not incompatible.

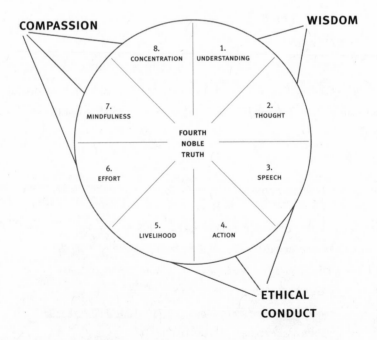

FIGURE 7.1: THE NOBLE EIGHTFOLD PATH

"[N]ature is not merely a collection of passive physical materials mutely waiting around to be dug up or chopped down, but is a dynamic, living system of plants, animals, soils, waters, weather, and numerous other processes that constitute the ultimate source of all our economic activities."

BARBARA BRANDT

8

WHAT PRICE THE BUDDHA?:
BUDDHISM, ECONOMICS, AND THE
INTERCONNECTED WORLD

IN *THE BREAKDOWN OF NATIONS,* Leopold Kohr argues that as communities and city-states became larger nations and embraced traditional Western economic thought, the illusion of material progress grew in importance. "Modern industrial workers," notes Kohr, "now produce in a week what took their eighteenth century counterpart four years." Of course, as industrial production has subsequently become massive, so has the cost of participating in it as a laborer and as a consumer.

Speaking to the fascination with economic size, Fritjof Capra points out in *The Turning Point* that as long as an "appropriate" size is not exceeded internally or externally, almost any organization (political or corporate) is likely to work, without the need to create significant control mechanisms. He also argues that when size becomes a problem, control mechanisms often turn out to be the unhealthiest elements in the administrative and creative operation of a holistic society or corporation. Small institutions have small problems, which are of human size, and can be handled by most individuals. But as institutions, both political and corporate, become larger, problems increase exponentially, as do instances of people and circumstances acting at cross-purposes. Therefore, as institutions increase in size, the effort to administer them must also increase.

Another perspective on size and economic enterprise is offered by Ernst Schumacher. Though not a Buddhist, Schumacher spent a considerable amount of time in Burma (now Myanmar) in the 1960s as an economic advisor to the Burmese government. In *Small Is Beautiful: Economics as if People Mattered,* he remarks on the ways in which communities developed using indigenous Buddhist practices. From these experiences, Schumacher concludes that people need to make a difference in their own economic lives, and that the only way they can do so is if the economic system in which they operate is within their capacity to influence. People need to understand and control the economics of their lives rather than living their whole lives with negligible impact on their circumstances.

Schumacher envisioned a society in which governments and economic systems are genuinely under human control, and where the size of institutions would be smaller than that of modern corporations. Built on a human scale, these would be more sensible, with a maximum of decentralized decision-making. The pace of change would be regulated not by the appetite for profit and power of an influential minority, but by the day-to-day needs of small-scale human communities and by the psychological capacities of community members to adapt.

This chapter offers a Buddhist perspective on economics—*free enterprise on a human scale*. We will begin by exploring the principles of organization in the natural world. This not only has implications for the size of institutions, but also provides instructive insights into the interconnectedness of all life. The implication is that the natural order of things can inform Western economic thought. This is the starting point for Buddhist economics. It has resonance for how we view our world and how we as corporations and individuals act in that world.

CONDITIONED ARISING

Environments, from ecosystems such as a seabed to organizations such as the companies within which we work, operate as complex systems. They are all constantly-evolving living systems, indistinguishable and inseparable from their occupants; and, at the same time, they are holistic systems with unique dynamic behaviors that develop and change over time.

The organizational dynamics that connect each of a company's parts—from the leaders themselves to the environment in which the business works—is in a constant state of change, always undergoing a complex process of evolution.

To draw an analogy from the natural world, we note that according to many modern scientists, such as Carl Sagan and David Suzuki, the natural biological response to such complexity and fluctuation has not historically been competition—as it is commonly assumed to have been, and as often is the case in the context of the corporate world—but cooperation. These scientists have posited that Darwin's original linear concept of evolution cannot fully explain the complexity and interconnectedness of life, and have not only shown us convincingly that evolution is much more likely a result of cooperation than competition, but have also described the kinds of methods and mechanisms used, for example, in the microbial world to share technology and machinery in order to build complexity. Indeed, it is likely that most of the simple microbiological cells that make up today's com-

> "It is clear that Buddhist economics must be very different from the economics of modern materialism, since the Buddhist sees the essence of civilization not in a multiplication of wants but in the purification of human character. Character, at the same time, is formed primarily by a [person's] work. And work, properly conducted in conditions of human dignity and freedom, blesses those who do it and equally their products." —Ernst Schumacher

plex cellular structures and our own DNA are more a result of a symbiotic interaction than of simple cellular machines that evolved independently. The microbial world uses these tools to bring about constancy in the environment and promote conditions supportive of life.

At the planetary level (the macro level), similarly complex and cooperative processes are also evident. Covering the earth's mantle is a "living web" of sentient beings and planetary elements. The earth, whose totality—the blue oceans, green and brown land masses, and white clouds—so awed the first astronauts, is quite literally alive. This living web has created dynamic conditions to ensure the earth's survival, guaranteeing, for example, a relative constancy of temperature over three to four billion years despite a thirty percent increase in the sun's radiation.

The systems view of life has come to realize that cooperation among all living systems has brought about this living mantle. Cooperation at the largest (planetary) and smallest (microbial) levels has created a web of life that has supported ever more complex and sophisticated forms of life, up to the present-day human species. Yet these life forms are all interconnected. They cannot exist in isolation.

There is a reason why I chose these specific systems for this analogy. These are living systems, with internal flexibility, whose functioning is controlled not by rigid mechanical structures, but by dynamic relations, properties of the dynamic principle of *self-organization* (see box). A living organism (a human being, for example) is a self-organizing system: its structure and function are not imposed solely by the environment but are established by the system itself. Self-organizing systems exhibit a certain degree

> Self-organizing systems are characterized by two dynamic phenomena:
> - *Self-renewal:* the ability to continuously renew and recycle their components while maintaining the integrity of their overall structure; and
> - *Self-transcendence:* the ability to reach out creatively beyond physical/mental/psychological boundaries to learn, develop, and evolve.

of autonomy. For example, they tend to establish their size according to internal principles of organization, independent of environmental influences. This does not mean that living systems are isolated from their environment; on the contrary, they interact with it continually, but this interaction does not solely determine their organization.

Not surprisingly, the principles of self-organization evident in the natural world also manifest themselves in our business practices. Most of us recognize the need to continually re-invest in the corporation (self-renewal) and the need to think "outside the box" (self-transcendence). The very fact that we are an evolving part of both our corporation and the marketplace in which we do business serves as further evidence of our interconnectedness, as we influence the marketplace by what we do, while the marketplace influences the nature of the corporation.

Our interconnectedness is crucial. The Vietnamese monk Thich Nhat Hanh refers to this special relationship as "interbeing." Self-organizing systems by their very nomenclature may sound autonomous. But the Buddha warned against an overblown view of what Western philosophy might call "free will." In an interconnected world, free will is limited and, at best, relative. Instead, the Buddha taught that any notion of a fully independent self is illusory, and advocated the transcendence of such a concept by becoming aware that we are inseparable parts of the cosmos in which we live.

SELF-ORGANIZING SYSTEMS

What can corporations operating in our current free enterprise environment learn from the natural order of things? Consider the following five principles, listed along with a few practical extrapolations:

1. *Growth and development come from cooperation rather than competition. There is interconnectedness between all beings.*

   ▶ The more a corporation works against this principle, the more it will create varying degrees of chaos within its own organization, and, if large enough, within the marketplace.

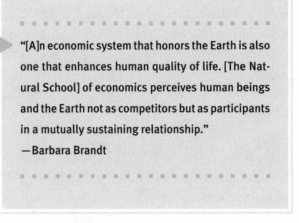

"[A]n economic system that honors the Earth is also one that enhances human quality of life. [The Natural School] of economics perceives human beings and the Earth not as competitors but as participants in a mutually sustaining relationship."
—Barbara Brandt

   ▶ No corporation, regardless of its size or influence, can survive in isolation.

   ▶ The more a corporation connects and co-operates with its stakeholders, the greater the likelihood of success.

   ▶ A corporation is a result of its culture and is shaped by its culture. Knowing the corporate culture and the guiding principles that support it helps ensure clarity, focus, and the potential for long-term growth. The products and services marketed by a corporation are a result of its culture.

2. *All life forms are self-organizing systems and the systems themselves establish their own structure and function.*

Self-organization means the ability to continuously renew (to avoid extinction) and the ability to transcend the individual's boundaries.

▶ For a corporation to survive it must go beyond the chaos in the marketplace (noting that some of the chaos is self-generated, and that the larger the corporation, the greater the chaos it will likely create).

▶ Viable and progressive corporations learn to transcend their own perceptions and fixed views, and realize that doing so does not undermine their viability. A modern bank would fail if it limited its self-identity to "banking" rather than "financial services" (along with all the additional businesses—investment, insurance, etc.—that implies). The older definition no longer applies.

3. *The Law of Cause and Effect, while a core teaching in Buddhism, is also a lesson from nature: "what goes around comes around."*

▶ Though a corporation is a legal entity, its guardians are the board of directors and senior executives. What these people do, or do not do, on behalf of the corporation sets in motion a chain reaction that always has consequences.

▶ If the guardians do wrong and break social conventions and/or the law, there will be a price to pay. This wrong action will inevitably lead, through some channel or other, to a negative consequence.

▶ To ignore the interconnectedness of all people can create outcomes beyond the guardians' expectations. Disregarding employees, and their relationship to each other and to the corporation, will result in employee turnover, alienation, and negative relationships with unions.

▶ To be insensitive to the needs of customers regarding quality products/services at fair prices will enable competitors to take your customers.

▶ Society, through its laws, has initiated a system to allow for the creation of corporations. To disregard the responsibility owed to the parent society will only lead to human suffering, in one form or another.

4. *There is always the opportunity to make choices.*

▶ Although corporations, through their guardians, exist to generate profit, those guardians should not assume that any or all stakeholders will continue to hold steadfastly and wholeheartedly to that narrow definition.

▶ For customers and employees to be loyal (a choice each makes for him or herself), there must be reciprocal behavior on the part of the corporation. One-sided relationships are doomed to the dustbin of corporate failure.

▶ To ensure that customers and employees *choose* to remain loyal, businesses need to *choose* to treat employees with respect and dignity, to provide safe, quality products/services, and to operate in an ethical, responsible manner.

5. *Size impacts every aspect of a living organism.*

▶ A large corporation cannot behave like a small family-operated business. Attempts to do so will eventually cause the corporation to divide into smaller organizations or lead to business failure.

▶ The larger the corporation, the greater the perceived need, by the guardians, to exercise control. This often generates significant infrastructure and can lead to a decline in personal commitment by employees and customers.

- ▶ Larger companies have more layers of management, which distances employees and customers from the "heart" of the system. (Small financial institutions such as credit unions talk about having "members," while larger banks have "customers.")
- ▶ Size can lead the guardians to illusions of grandeur and jeopardize the corporation's viability.

BUDDHIST ECONOMICS

How then do we integrate the lessons of the natural world into our economic and business practices? How should we incorporate the notions of size, complexity, and interconnectedness that Capra, Schumacher, and others have advocated? The answer is what I will call Buddhist economics—though I acknowledge up front my debt to the school of Natural Economics (which we discussed in Chapter 4).

Buddhist economics, as articulated by Schumacher, is not an economic concept in the traditional sense, but rather an idea: a program to be filled in by others as they become enthusiastic about this cause. Recall the example of the Sarvodaya Movement that we discussed previously. What Dr. Ari T. Ariyaratne demonstrates through Sarvodaya is that economic arguments are *not* scientific arguments. Instead, economics are a discourse on the agreements that govern people pursuing their human productive and distributive activities in society.

That there can even be a notion of Buddhist economics follows from the Guiding Principle of Skillful Livelihood, one of the lessons of the Buddha's Fourth Noble Truth, the Noble Eightfold Path. This Guiding Principle embodies Causing No Harm—to sentient beings or to the environment—in its most inclusive sense. Because people must live, and live skillfully, they must resolve their economic needs without causing suffering.

The keynotes of Buddhist economics are simplicity, ecology, and non-violence. From a Natural Economist's point of view, the marvel of the Buddhist way of life is its simplicity. Schumacher called this "amazingly small means leading to extraordinarily satisfactory results." From the perspective of Buddhist economics, the purpose of economic life is to obtain a maximum of well-being with a minimum of consumption. This means that producing locally for local or community needs is the most rational economy.

The teachings of the Buddha counsel a reverent and non-violent attitude toward not only all sentient beings but also nature as a whole.

On the other hand, generally speaking, modern economic practice in the industrialized world has little regard for whether or not a resource is renewable and for the state of the environment after productive activity has taken place. To live off the capital of a non-renewable resource rather than on renewable energy is essentially parasitic. A traditional economist, for example, would look at statistics showing an increase in the number of gallons of diesel fuel used to transport goods from manufacturers to consumers as proof of economic progress, as more goods are making their way to market. A Buddhist economist, on the other hand, would view the same calculations as a highly undesirable escalation in consumption and its resulting negative impact on the environment.

THE INDIVIDUAL WITHIN THE ECONOMIC

An individual's paycheck is required to meet the four basic necessities of life: food and water, shelter, clothing, and medicine. Additional income can support other needs, including the need to be generous and compassionate to those less fortunate. If, however, additional income seduces us into unnecessary materialism and consumerism, valuable time—the true benefit of additional income—will be taken away from our moral, ethical, and spiritual development.

The Buddhist assessment of free enterprise then has important implications for the individual. The inevitability of globalization is that hundreds of thousands of jobs flow to where labor costs are the lowest. There is a qualified benefit to the less developed nations in this transfer, but what about those left unemployed in their home country? A corporation who has thought through the human costs of their outsourcing initiatives—let alone acted on such considerations by seeking out other options—is the rare exception. Since our present economic system does not respond to people's welfare holistically, the ranks of those living at the poverty line and those being made redundant constantly increases.

The division of labor inherent to capitalism is consistently dehumanizing. Tasks become so menial and insignificant that the individual has no hope of expressing his or her human potential through them. Through the influence of such men as Henry Ford and Frederick Taylor—the twentieth century's champions of the disconnect between human values and employment—"joy" in the workplace has become the exception and not the rule.

The traditional economics view that work is associated with

dissatisfaction, foreign to previous ages but painfully obvious in early-industrialized countries, is now emerging in the developing world. When Natural Economists assert that work has a humanizing function, it is not proposing something new, but reaffirming

> ### THE IMPLICIT VALUES OF A VALUE-FREE MARKET
>
> When traditional Western economists assert that economics is value-free, or is a system where human values do not interfere with the operation of the market, they are arguing that it is economically acceptable, for example, to:
>
> - Pay the lowest possible wages, thus exploiting many employed people;
> - Design work in such a way that repetitive or meaningless job activities are all too often the norm;
> - Let there be unemployed people in the world's wealthiest countries; and
> - Consider people disposable—the collateral damage of globalization, the current free enterprise system.

an idea about community that existed before the Industrial Age. And this complements the Buddhist perspective, in which work, besides providing a livelihood, serves three purposes:

▶ To enable men and women to develop their talents, skills, competencies, etc.;

▶ To allow them to overcome their ego-centeredness by joining with others in a common task; and

▶ To create and produce the goods and services needed for the existence of both individuals and society.

I would argue that creating work that satisfies these needs and also generates acceptable financial rewards is not impossible. In a different time and distant place, the Buddha taught that the inclusion of three factors in an economic system leads to a society being stable and healthy:

The First Factor addresses earnings or income through skillful and earnest means—through endeavors that are morally and ethically just and encompass one's total being. The Buddha cautioned us against the tendency to accumulate wealth for its own sake, arguing that this would lead to both physical and mental suffering later on in this or our next life. Following the Buddha's Middle Way—an adequate livelihood to support ourselves and our families, to assist relatives and friends, and to provide financial support to the needy and deserving—leads to contentment and inner satisfaction. This, in turn, results in the moral and spiritual advancement of individuals, and, eventually, of society as a whole.

Although there is a clear connection here with the equitable distribution of wealth and its resulting benefits for society, Buddhism is focused on individual growth and development— each must end his or her own suffering. This First Factor, therefore, clearly places the onus for one's own welfare on the individual and not on the state or corporations. The idea is to look after one's own needs and the needs of those less fortunate, keeping in mind the Buddhist understanding of karma: generosity results in goodness, whereas excess results in more suffering.

The Second Factor addresses the physical or worldly satisfaction derived from knowing that one's investments and sources of income are protected from obvious material damage (theft, fire, etc.). Consistent with protection is prudence about going into debt, in order to avoid the sufferings of unmanageable debt and the resulting distractions and pain it causes.

In one of his lessons the Buddha suggested to a wealthy merchant that he should divide his income and investments into four parts. These should be distributed so that one part would be used for the family's daily living, one part for the operation of a business, one part given for those in need, and the final part set aside for emergencies. Again, the underlying goal is to be prudent while protecting one's income for basic needs, while developing one's business energetically.

> "The forces of a capitalist economy, if left unchecked, tend to make the rich richer and the poor poorer."
> —Jawaharlal Nehru

The Third Factor addresses the Buddha's concept of a simple life. Simplicity is a virtue because it allows the individual time to develop his or her mind. The more complete this development, the greater the likelihood that the individual will understand the true causes of suffering and be able to turn toward joy. The idea is to lead a simple life, to enjoy the love of family and friends, the experience of nature, and to save financially for the inevitable illnesses and emergencies.

Leading a life with less materialism and less consumerism—a simpler life—results in less mental clutter and more time available to devote to a not-so-simple process: the development of one's mind.

WHAT THE INDIVIDUAL CAN DO

The environment in which business operates is an evolving system. The Buddhist view of economics—which encourages us to live a simple life within institutions of natural, manageable size—enables us to consider individual action within an economic life. To begin reducing our reliance on material things for happiness and making constructive change to our society by adding human values, all we need to do, I believe, is to appreciate the influence we have over our economic system and ourselves.

Our objective is to modify the system—and even small changes can ripple outward in ways beyond our precise imagination to have larger and larger effects. One very simple act you can take today is to contact your financial institution and ask them to buy a stock, bond, or mutual fund that is an "ethical" or "green" investment. You may not get an immediate result, but the message will begin to get out: we are balancing the importance of the environment and the interconnectedness of all life with our need to maximize short-term financial gain.

Our economy is comprised of constituents who all work for a common set of goals: profit, growth, and, in the worst-case scenario, business survival at any cost. The link between profit and business growth creates a symbiotic relationship between investors and executives. For with no capital brought in by the investor, there is no business to manage; and with no enterprise, there is no return-on-investment.

Nature shows us that symbiotic relationships, which are

mutually gratifying, generally have very strong ties and interwoven dependencies. If the relationship proves to be mutually profitable there is little, if any, motivation to change it. If the relationship is unsatisfactory for either or both partners, they move on.

To put human values into the economic mix, we need to begin first by re-evaluating all our purchasing decisions and supporting those manufacturers and service providers who clearly demonstrate their support for human values and the environment; and second by assessing the consequences of each purchase—how will this purchase affect the quality of human life now and in the future?

Most of all, we need to believe that we are important, that we can change ourselves, that we can Cause No Harm, and that we can influence our communities. These issues may seem outside the realm of capitalism, but they are at the heart of the economic system. If we lose confidence in who we are and follow the crowd in all our purchasing decisions, we will be giving in to mass marketing and consumerism at its worst.

Better to remember our integration in the world and in the cosmic pattern and to believe in our own inherent self-worth and goodness.

9

MOVING BEYOND THE BOTTOM LINE:
BUDDHIST ETHICS AND BUSINESS

BUDDHISM does not see economics as an isolated topic but rather as a field that merges with ethics (how we relate to others and life's difficult questions) and links to our spirituality (our connection with our mind/body and with all living beings and nature). As with the Buddhist perspective on economics, Buddhist ethics for the boardroom offers lessons for both corporate practices and individual behavior.

ETHICAL BEHAVIOR

Ethics can be difficult to catalog and codify, despite the increasing popularity of statements of ethical business practices.

Too often jargon such as the recently popular "triple bottom line" (profit plus the well-being of people plus the health of the environment) is used only as public-relations exercises that are only wedded to a company's financial targets and reflect no real deep-seated commitments to global well-being. While perhaps not unethical (and even this may be a generous assessment), the substitution of such marketing stand-ins for corporate ethics is certainly disingenuous. It obscures a genuine discussion of business ethics.

From a legal and corporate perspective, unethical behavior can include the actions banned in our human rights, employment, and health and safety legislation; the manufacturing and/or selling of defective products; and bribery or any other unlawful acts covered by civil or criminal legislation. From a Buddhist perspective, however, unethical behavior goes beyond the laws of society to include mental intentions and their subsequent actions. Meditation is an effective tool for being able to explore deeply all of our intentions.

ETHICS AT WORK

If we disregard, for a moment, all the advertising and public relations hype, we can differentiate among businesses based on their values systems.

To explore this, join me on the following thought experiment. Let's say you work as a Production Manager for a paint manufacturer who still uses lead in its oil-based paint. The paint is sold into the developing world to paint children's toys. The toys are then sold—again in the developing world, where the children who play with them chew on their toys (as children do everywhere). Some get sick. Some die. As a middle manager you were not aware of these events. All related reports were kept in the corporation's legal department. The corporation is sued. After learning of the settlement, you ask about your personal responsibility and accountability in this case. You ask because you do not feel right about what happened. Your conscience is troubled.

Within the management team, you perform your job responsibilities well. Your manager, the VP of Manufacturing, is quite satisfied with your work, but you still are not comfortable with what happened. The company hid information about the export of their products, about the children who were made ill, and later, about the death of the children. Every time you think about the children who died, you remember that they could have been your children. But no, they could not have been your children, because our country has laws prohibiting the use of lead-based paint on children's toys. There are no laws that cover the exporting of such products, however. And there are no laws covering painted children's toys in developing countries.

How would you see your doubts about the handling of this incident? Do you feel empathy or personal pain for the parents who lost children? Does your experience tell you that the court settlement, thought to be excessive by the company, will not have any long-term effect on the executives' decision to continue exporting lead-based paint? Are you sensing that this incident affected you more than most other business transactions? Perhaps you realize you feel a loss, as though you need time to grieve?

The First Noble Truth says "life includes suffering." The Second Noble Truth tells us that there are causes for all suffering and that the causes are related to our attachments. Since you are suffering as an outcome of this tragedy, you must be attached to something. To what are you attached, though? The lack of caring shown by the executive team for the children who died? Corporate practices that in our home country would run contrary to the company's Values and Mission statements? The double standard that places greater value on profit than on well-being? A sense of the injustice at the fact that this situation will likely not change regardless of how much money is paid out by the company? Your moral reaction to seeing that you were in some way complicit and that your actions contributed to the events that took place?

Attachment to this incident does not have to come from a single source; it can emerge from a whole series of events. And, just as there can be multiple potential sources of the attachment, the many sources of our perceptions can bring new ideas and experiences to our mind. But it is not until we recognize and understand that there is an attachment that we can respond to it.

Let us assume that the attachment in this case is to the injustice of the fact that the executive group will not change either the paint formulation or the marketing of the paint to toy manufacturers in less developed countries. Additional illnesses and deaths are a real possibility. The mindfulness that led you to this conclusion is a positive step in understanding the suffering you are going through. Mindfulness also leads you to understand the interdependence between you, the company, and the children. The question is what to do next? Buddhism would suggest you seek a deeper understanding of the Five Precepts. The deeper your understanding of these principles, the more likely you are to act to alleviate the suffering of others, because you find your own suffering is inextricably linked with theirs.

Such an experience and the insights it brings into the nature of suffering, attachment, and ethical responses need not be limited to the level of the individual—they can (and hopefully will) reverberate across an organization.

VALUES AND CORPORATE ETHICS STATEMENTS

To articulate an organization's values system is not a simple task. It is not unusual for one of my clients to request a two- or three-day retreat to facilitate a discussion that helps their organization to clarify its values. Most often, the process cannot be completed in such a short time—there are too many unresolved issues. Too many important ideas are left unspoken, and the link between personal and corporate values has not been thoroughly explored.

Because retreats are usually held during good economic times, the output of the retreat will be a document which unfortunately has no relationship to what the values statement might look like if the retreat had occurred in bad economic times. Too often, the good intentions underpinning corporate values and guiding principles are thrown to the wind when unexpected opportunities present themselves or when profitability is in question. This act of "throwing to the wind" the corporation's supposed principles then becomes the real core value.

Values statements prepared by corporations were not that popular twenty-five or thirty years ago (though there were some notable exceptions such as the Johnson & Johnson Credo, mentioned in Chapter 2). After all, why publish anything that might restrict our business options in the future?

But times have changed (as all things do) and most major national and transnational corporations have now published Values and/or Mission Statements. These documents describe, in broad terms, the business's vision, mission, and goals ("to be North America's leading producer of quality widgets"), and the values and guiding principles to be followed in achieving them ("maximize shareholder's return," "our customer is the driver,"

In a recent article in the Hsi Lai Journal of Humanistic Buddhism, Otto Chang, Ph.D., suggests the following twelve ethical principles from which a universal set of business ethics can be constructed:

- Business should obey all the laws in the international community and directives of various governments, domestic and foreign.
- Business should respect all people and cultures it encounters in carrying out its operations.
- Business should align its mission and goals with its social responsibilities of advancing human civilization, and plan its overall strategies accordingly, to promote education, morality, and social welfare.
- Business should adopt technology friendly to the environment and least harmful to humans and animals.
- Business should produce goods that are safe to consume, and disclose fully potential risks of using the products.
- Business should use its economic resources efficiently and recycle any reusable materials to save natural resources.

"cutting-edge technologies," "we treat employees with respect," and so on).

If the message inherent in these values is to be meaningful and form the basis for the direction of strategic decisions, they must be an expression of holistic understanding. Corporations are based on more than just numbers. They need creativity and innovation. The substance of these types of values becomes what the company will tenaciously hold on to in both good times and bad. It's the company's ethical (i.e., non-financial) performance

- Business should treat its employees with respect, empower them in decision-making, reward them appropriately, and help them achieve their career and life goals.
- Business should provide a work environment free from any type of discrimination and/or harassment.
- Business should establish appropriate corporate governance structures and processes to ensure the interest of all its stakeholders are not infringed by the management.
- Business should not use exploitative strategies to deplete economic resources of foreign countries or monopolistic measures to wipe out competition.
- Business should not engage in false advertising and aggressive marketing strategies that are harmful to the society.
- Business should invest in human and economic capital, and conduct research and development to advance productivity, technology, and human knowledge. *(Reprinted by permission)*

in bad times that separates a realistic and liveable Values Statement from one that is just a public-relations exercise or marketing slogan.

Most of today's progressively minded organizations create for each of their values a set of guiding behaviors. These guiding behaviors let each stakeholder, especially leaders and employees, know what is acceptable and what is unacceptable in *living* the Values Statement. Corporately developed guiding behaviors reflect the values of that specific organization; the

Buddha's Eight Guiding Principles can be seen as universal to individuals and corporations that wish to Cause No Harm.

This distinction between company-specific and malleable corporate values and the inviolable, unchanging truths of the Noble Eightfold Path is important. In my professional experience the exercise to develop guiding behaviors receives mixed reviews. Though there may be good intentions at the outset, bad economic times have the effect of focusing leaders' attention on a single number—the bottom line. The Values exercise, as important as it is, unfortunately takes root in very few cases, as values are regularly overruled by unforeseen circumstances and as new CEOs introduce different agendas. When push comes to shove, a profit-and-loss statement will almost always outrank a values statement. This betrayal of the values statement is usually accompanied with a good dose of rationalization, thereby reshaping the company's ethical reality. Because today's iteration of capitalism is singularly focused on profit, it would be naïve to expect a different response.

We learn about a person's or company's values from the actions they take on behalf of their beliefs—not from attractively packaged Values and Mission Statements posted in executive wings and corporate lobbies. And this is where the crux of the values problem occurs. Corporate values are meaningless unless the people who *are* the corporation apply them.

It is we as individuals, and not the legal entity called a corporation, who have the capacity and the responsibility for ethical behavior. Values, and the living of values, do count.

"Intention is everything; all else is consequence."
BUDDHIST ADAGE

10

THE HEALTHY ORGANIZATION

SOME OF THE PRACTICES and behaviors of modern corporations that make them, in the Buddhist view of the world, unhealthy organizations, were outlined in Chapter 2. I want to return to that label—"unhealthy"—and reconsider it in light of the skillful behaviors of the Guiding Principles of the Noble Eightfold Path.

We'll do that by looking at one specific stakeholder group within organizations—employees. Moreover, we will consider organizations from both sides of Western industrial relations: management and unions. After thirty years of dealing with companies and their issues related to unionization, I have seen plenty of unskillful behavior on both sides of this divide.

The important lesson to take away from this discussion is the value of *self-responsibility*. Healthy organizations create such a climate for their employees. And this means more than giving employees *choice* in the workplace (choice in work processes, job design, etc.). It also calls for the ownership of one's responsibilities and the consequences that follow from one's choices.

SKILLFUL LIVELIHOOD IN THE WORKPLACE

It is unfortunate that, as business leaders, we both knowingly and unknowingly ask employees to give up many of their choices and personal direction over their intentions. It seems to be part of the package deal called "being an employee": Check your values at the door when you enter—and, in too many cases (particularly in production-line manufacturing jobs), check your mind as well.

On the one hand, leaders know they cannot do everything by themselves; on the other, they want employees to do what they are told. This creates a "Catch 22" for employees. If they do what they are told to do, they appear to show little or no initiative or drive to do their job more efficiently or innovatively. When employees see the big picture and, on their own initiative, look for better ways to achieve their jobs' objectives, they are frequently portrayed as "free thinkers" or, worse, undisciplined trouble-makers. These are examples of unhealthy leadership perceptions that inevitably cause harm to many stakeholders.

Managerial practices such as these will change in organizations that see the Guiding Principle of Skillful Livelihood as the path to follow. To develop a culture that supports this, an organization must reassess the relationships it has with employees against the criteria established by all eight of the Guiding Principles. Not to do so will lead management to revert to traditional beliefs: "a fair day's pay for a fair day's work," or the view that employees are disposable and can be discarded at the whim of the employer, as merely a means to an end.

In this environment, leaders will want to offer employees the opportunity to be creative and to think through problems from different perspectives. Creativity and the ensuing commitment it brings are qualities that frequently make the difference between successful and unsuccessful organizations. If obedience is the outcome of following orders and creativity is the outcome of free thinking, we will only achieve our overarching value of Causing No Harm through the latter effort. For an employer to support this Guiding Principle, the organization will need to create and champion a culture that encourages and empowers individuals and groups to discover the causes of suffering and then work toward reducing and eliminating these causes.

This means there is a direct connection between how an employer has designed work and what an employee retains from performing that work. The simpler and more routine a job or set of work tasks is, the less the individual can creatively engage with their work. This not only leads to an unhealthy work environment, it completely misses the opportunity to let individuals grow as human beings while performing at higher levels of potential.

The opportunity presented by Skillful Livelihood is one of self-discovery for all employees. It can substitute innovation for drudgery and add value to one's life journey. It creates an opportunity for all employees to discover their own wisdom and compassion. This is "Causing No Harm" in the workplace.

In a workplace guided by positive intentions around Causing No Harm, we will find a people-oriented culture, a setting that is values- and relationship-driven, and employees who believe they are in a nurturing environment where their competencies, capabilities, and commitment are respected, encouraged, and appreciated.

When employers choose not to follow this path, the organization will become unhealthy. There will be high turnover, the best performers will continue to leave, there will be an ever-increasing demand for more money, and a sense of mediocrity will prevail. The traditional approach of trying to smooth the waters through damage control that throws money at the situation just does not work. These are stopgap fixes, not solid, values-based solutions.

However, an employer's motivation for changing such a paradigm should not be simply to gain a more productive work force. *If the employer's intentions are only productivity oriented, then he or she is acting in an unskillful manner and will ultimately be causing harm.*

We began this chapter with the Buddhist axiom that intention is everything and that all else is consequence. Translated to the workplace this means that the two-way employment relationship is based on intentions. The more positive the intentions on the part of both parties the stronger the relationship. A strong relationship is characterized by mutual respect and a commitment to perform the job to the best of one's current abilities. This means that both parties to the relationship understand that:

- ▶ employment is not a lifetime arrangement (unless both parties agree to this as time goes on);
- ▶ upward mobility is not guaranteed and is not seen as the substantive issue (instead, the substantive issue is considered to be harmonized positive values); and
- ▶ leadership styles based on paternalism (which, in reality, is sugar-coated autocratic behavior) never lead to personal growth and self-development.

Employees, I believe, will embrace positive actions with the proviso that leaders are fair, honest, and open about their support for the value of Causing No Harm. Provided this value is clearly communicated, it should be evident that it applies to employees just as much as it does to every other stakeholder. To demonstrate this integrity, leaders will need to change their beliefs about their roles and responsibilities, their attitudes toward employees, and the way management creates and designs work.

Work can be liberating activity if leaders create a culture of self-awareness and personal growth. Liberating work does not depend on someone's role or responsibilities; it depends on the individual employee and how he or she views the act of working. The more disconnected we as individuals feel from our work, the more feelings of insecurity and discontent will continue. It is very

> **"It is beneath human dignity to lose one's individuality and become a mere cog in the machine."**
> —Mahatma Gandhi

difficult to give up negative attachments when one works in an unhealthy environment.

In light of the Buddhist idea that *how profit is earned is more important than the actual profit,* it is well within the responsibilities of any leader to see his or her role as that of trainer, mentor, and facilitator. It is the wise and compassionate leader who can assist employees to see that whatever they are doing now, this very moment is not a moment of discontent; it is a moment of fulfillment—for this is the only moment of reality.

From a Buddhist perspective, Robert Rosen's five characteristics of trustworthiness (see box on page 142) are the building blocks of becoming a wise leader. We can create an environment where Skillful Livelihood will flourish once we earn the employees' trust and use that trust with positive intentions. Employees want more understanding, compassion, and self-development opportunities at work, as well as more enlightened attitudes and behaviors from all leaders. (See the "employee's charter of rights" box for an example of a path toward this goal.)

An "employee's charter of rights" would probably include the following:

- Respect our beliefs.
- Respect our diversity.
- Respect our need to be involved.
- Respect our need for skill and personal development.
- Respect our need for a healthy and supportive workplace.
- Respect us holistically as spiritual beings.
- Respect us by showing leadership based in trust, wisdom, and compassion.

UNIONS AND SELF-RESPONSIBILITY

As a consultant, I would argue that unions today exist primarily because of the unskillful decisions and actions of corporate leaders. The *raison d'être* of trade unions is to improve wages, benefits, and working conditions for their members. It could be argued, without stretching the point too far, that they are the consequences of negative karma resulting from corporate greed.

Harmful and self-serving employment practices, resulting from unskillful intentions, lead to negative relations with unions. A skillful employer, however, using human-resources practices grounded in the values of what I have called elsewhere Positive Employee Relations, would likely receive much more positive feedback from the employee group—perhaps to the point where employees might decide they do not need a union to represent their interests.

At one time, unions were the sole source of trades-related education. Guilds in medieval Europe performed, at least conceptually, a similar function to present-day community colleges and apprenticeship programs. Historically, unions have had significant influence over what constituted a trade and how individuals, primarily through apprenticeships, learned that trade. From the beginning of the Industrial Revolution, the union movement fought to protect factory labor, often immigrants, from long hours, dreadful working conditions, and meager pay. Despite these origins, unions today are as susceptible to negative intentions as any other organization. Just like the leaders of any organization, leaders of unions are capable of unskillful intentions, actions, and behaviors.

Unions as a whole suffer from the same attachments as the individuals who create and manage them. Like a corporation, a union operates within the free-enterprise system and is just as prone to fostering excesses—the Three Poisons of greed, hatred, and delusion—as is unrestricted capitalism. A union, like a corporation, is interested in the bottom line. The reality is that unions, like corporations, are legal entities—they enter into contracts, they can be sued, and they can initiate legal actions—but the values of the union are the values of the people who created or control the union.

In *The Healthy Company,* Robert Rosen argues that trust-worthiness can be divided into five characteristics:

- *Credibility:* The quality and believability of the leader's word.
- *Dependability:* Doing what you said you would do (without exception unless clearly explaining why; to not do so leads to indifference).
- *Predictability:* Being consistent in ensuring open communication and following the idea that employees, just like leaders, do not like surprises.
- *Valuing the Common Good:* Demonstrating the ability to put aside self-interest for the good of the team, customer, etc.
- *Emotional Safety:* Valuing everyone's health (physical and emotional), self-image, and belief systems with compassion and wisdom.

Unions sell their services to employees and then act on their behalf to negotiate employment terms and conditions with the employer. In over thirty years of human-resources experience, both in-house and as a consultant, I have never encountered a trade unionist that did not see his or her union as anything other than a paragon of democracy. The unionist would argue that from the beginning of the organizing process, through negotiating and signing a collective agreement, and then working to protect employee rights under the terms and conditions of the contract, every part of the process is open to the public (or at least available for inspection by the members) and all important decisions are taken to the membership for approval. One could quickly be misled to believe that unions *only* exist to protect the rights of their members.

My perception of the reality of labor relations is somewhat different. Union leaders are no more or less ethical than their corporate counterparts. We must remember, when we consider the rhetoric of union idealism, the dues (and sometimes the fines) that are deducted from its members' paychecks each month. Unions are in the business of business and their decisions are not necessarily driven by either benevolence or integrity. (Union members may not be fully aware of this, or they may suffer from their own delusion regarding the roles their unions play in the employee-employer relationship.)

Consider for a moment a different perspective on unions, one which takes self-responsibility as its starting point. Self-responsibility is a significant component of the Buddha's message. Understanding our cravings—desires that arise from our interpretation of our feelings, thoughts, and intentions (whether conscious or unconscious)—and how these cravings influence our intentions is how we begin to take responsibility for our actions, behaviors, and our suffering.

From this perspective it should be clear that no one can delegate to a service provider his or her personal responsibility to be ethical and still be considered to be taking self-responsibility. A personal agent cannot follow and apply the Guiding Principles for any individual's benefit. To assume that a union can be a surrogate for one's own perseverance in holding to the Middle Way is an illusion.

On becoming a member of a union, an employee does not

necessarily learn self-responsibility with the goal of becoming more responsible for his or her own intentions and actions, to subsequently leave the union a wiser and more compassionate person. Unions thrive on the problems of their members. If there were no problems to resolve, there would be no need for a union. The methods unions use to resolve problems are in part designed to gain more credibility with members and to demonstrate to management that they have an ever-increasing base of power and influence. To be a union member is to be a consumer, and no enterprise wants to sell its services and never see its customers again.

To carry this point one step further, if a union member wishes to leave the union, he or she will likely lose his or her job. Most collective agreements cover all the employees in a particular bargaining unit and if one were to resign from the union, he or she could not continue to be employed as a non-union employee. Unions clearly do not thrive on teaching self-responsibility to their members. They allow them the democratic choice to leave the union but not the democratic choice to become a non-unionized employee with the same employer. In fact, the more individuals learn to rely on a union to solve their problems for them, the stronger that union becomes and the weaker the employees' self-resolve becomes.

Given the largely unrestricted free enterprise environment in which corporations conduct their business affairs, it is inconceivable that unions will unilaterally change their strategies. The history of industrial-relations is not the history of either the corporation or the union. It is the history of how the two have *interacted*. All too often this interaction has been the result of unskillful intentions (and subsequent unskillful actions and behaviors) on both sides. The competitive and inherently adversarial nature of Western culture will just breed more of the same. Frequently union-management relations epitomize the Buddha's definition of suffering caused by attachments.

As long as corporations treat their employees as disposable, unions will have no incentive to seek out alternative values systems for their movement. Likewise, as long as unions, in the supposed best interests of their members, cause suffering for corporations, employers have no incentive to seek out other values systems. Unions and corporations are joined at the bottom line. Their respective strategies and tactics are an expression of the same system in which they both operate. The economic justification for both unions and corporations is the profit motive.

The industrial relations model in North America is based on an adversarial system that has workplace disruption as one of its key strategic options. A strike or lockout is the last step in the process, the one that shows that negotiations, and sometimes political posturing, have failed to result in a mutually agreeable solution. Despite its "last resort" status, it is worth noting that, historically, work stoppages rarely result in unions regaining their members' lost income.

In looking for alternatives to resolve labor-management disagreements, we need to see this relationship from a different perspective. A relationship built on collaboration would not necessarily have the strike/lockout option as the last stage or even as an alternative at all. If the driving forces of greed and hatred were removed, business and union leaders would be able to engage in an entirely new discourse. If the Guiding Principles of the Noble Eightfold Path were to underpin union and management industrial-relations practices, creative and alternative problem-solving methods would present themselves to both parties. (Indeed, if the Guiding Principles were being used as the Buddha recommended, employees would not need union representation in the first place.)

Operating in an adversarial environment means that, from the outset, both parties acknowledge that their negotiations will have a winner and a loser. Words such as *adversary, threat, disruption,* and *force* are the currently acceptable mode of discourse for union-management relations. It should be clear how the Buddha's message about causing suffering—the hurtfulness of negative intentions, the suffering-causing karma of ill-will—typifies relations between the parties. This suffering is frequently sustained by acts of unskillful action and speech as well as unethical behavior.

Could the Guiding Principles be the foundation for a trade union? I think the answer to this question lies more with the unrestricted nature of our free-enterprise system than it does with the nature of unions. *If shareholders and investors, like you and me, raise the importance of Creating a Better Society to a position of parity with profit, then we will naturally begin to change the free-enterprise model.* People and profits will be given equal rating on corporate financial statements. By evolving toward a more "just society," the suffering corporations cause employees will be dramatically reduced. Once the well-being of individuals and society becomes a priority, unions will also be encouraged and be able to operate with a different values system. We could then ask the question, "Are unions still needed?"

HEALTHY HIRING

Although employees are clearly not "owned" by the employer, companies may refer to their employees as "assets" to suggest that they are truly valued. But such language can also reflect a patronizing approach that has glitter but little substance.

I propose that a managerial model that assumes that people are assets is fundamentally flawed. People *partner with* organizations to satisfy the needs that both have. Employment is a two-way relationship between people performing different roles. From the days of Adam Smith and the origins of modern capitalism, this was intended to be a mutually beneficial relationship.

But when these two employment needs, candidate/partner and employer, come together, unfortunately the relationship is frequently *not* based on respect, trust, and compassion. From the time the employment decision is made, the employer usually has about 80 percent of the available information while the prospective employee has only 20 percent. How could a candidate conduct reference checks on his/her future manager, let alone obtain a copy of the manager's resumé? This is a strange way to start a relationship based on mutual respect and trust.

Valuing a partner implies a willingness on the part of the employer to acknowledge that the employee needs comparable information so that he/she can make as knowledgeable an employment decision as the employer. This step alone would turn current human resources practices on their head. The employee would be in fact, and not just in words, a partner in the employment relationship.

This is what applied Buddhist practice could bring to the healthy organization.

SECTION 4: PRESCRIPTION

WALKING THE PATH

"Enlightened management is one way of taking religion seriously, profoundly, deeply, and earnestly."
ABRAHAM MASLOW

11

MEASURING SUCCESS:
THE TRANSITION TO COMPASSION

IT IS A REALITY that we all must work to earn income for our needs: housing, food, clothing, health care, education, etc. In an ideal setting, our employment choices are influenced by at least two critical factors: first, our ability to skillfully choose job responsibilities that adhere to the Guiding Principles and the Five Precepts; and second, the availability of employment opportunities that are themselves grounded in these Principles and Precepts.

As a consultant, however, I have seen the predominant reality. Front-line employees, working within the constraints of *unrestricted* free enterprise that thrives on greed and excess, must, to meet their basic income needs, accept mindless tasks in workplaces where the ethical standards are at best value-neutral and where pride is taken in meeting only the minimum requirements of labor legislation. It is not until society begins to acknowledge, in human terms, the negative impact of *unrestricted* free enterprise on the well-being of individuals and communities that leaders will begin to feel empowered to skillfully modify our ever-changing economic system. Indeed, there are people in executive positions who are working toward these changes today.

The decade-old movement known as "Corporate Social Responsibility" is, in effect, an attempt to contribute to the goal of Creating a Better Society.

This chapter is about acknowledging that the individual journeys that we take along the spiritual path can have profound consequences for the workplaces we inhabit. While the journey is a personal one, its lessons can be realized in our work lives—and I will offer some initial steps to begin this journey. As business leaders we can help create more compassionate workplaces; environments where success goes well beyond the bottom line and where joyful, enriching work is not merely some platitude hung on the wall in Human Resources, but is the lived reality of employees throughout the organization.

CHANGE IS OUR RESPONSIBILITY

The Buddha argued that for a society to be healthy, the individuals who make up the society must also be healthy. Societal well-being is then fundamentally a bottom-up process. It is through pursuing our own self-understanding and well-being that we can assist others. Governments or corporations, for example, cannot make us healthy, give us insight, or help us detach from the Three Poisons. This we must do for ourselves, and then we can help those closest to us, and then more and more others. (However, having governments and/or the judicial system more involved in the physical and emotional safety of society—relating to crime, illicit drugs, business malpractice, etc.—would be a positive initiative.)

The goal of Buddhism is to see individuals at peace with themselves, free from cravings and attachments, and accepting of the impermanent nature of existence—in other words, free from suffering. This "at peace" means that individuals are responsible for their own state of mind—it is not the responsibility of governments or employers to make this happen—though as history has shown, these institutions can certainly influence such growth either skillfully or unskillfully.

We begin to articulate our vision of a healthy society by embracing ethical conduct and compassion, not by earning greater profits. Indeed, as the wisdom that emanates from the Four Noble Truths becomes more widely understood, other individuals may choose to follow this Path. This people-focused definition of societal change is rooted in the pursuit of inner peace and the equanimity of individuals and not in the belief that an entity outside of ourselves can bring about change. The first step in Creating a Better Society is acknowledging that *we are the change!*

MONEY AND ETHICS

The Buddha's teachings compel us to incorporate our new-found personal awareness regarding intentions, ethical behavior, and compassion into our work lives. In very real ways, the executive, managerial, and professional class in Western society constitutes the world's most affluent group of consumers. With their purchasing power they set national and global business agendas. Within the free-enterprise system, this group sets the ethical bar. The most influential among them reinforce unrestricted free enterprise, place consumerism above most other things, and influence trends and technologies so that consumers are always buying to keep up.

Money, any currency, any denomination, is just a system to represent the value of work, worth, and exchange. The reality is that money does nothing on its own initiative. Money in and of itself has no value; it only has the value that we all agree to give it. Because money is the vehicle to purchase something, anything,

> The World Business Council for Sustainable Development defines Corporate Social Responsibility as, "the continuing commitment by business to behave ethically and contribute to economic development while improving the quality of life of the workforce and their families as well as of the local community and society at large." The American delegation at a 1999 regional meeting of the World Business Council in Detroit, where 170 international companies were represented, went on to say, "Corporate Social Responsibility is about taking personal responsibility for your actions and the impacts that you have on society. Companies and employees must undergo a personal transformation, re-examine their roles, their responsibilities and increase the level of accountability."

we attribute to it properties—being the source of happiness or a symbol of status—that it does not intrinsically have.

Money has no say in how it is earned, saved, spent, or invested. Rather, these are choices that we make. To be mindful about money is to be mindful of the choices we make. Problems arise, I would argue, when money becomes the *only* barometer for value (or happiness) in our society. The illusion is to believe that money equals happiness, or for that matter that money equals anything other than an accepted medium of exchange.

To be mindful of our earnings, we need to examine our intentions and the cause-and-effect consequences involved in:

- ▶ Work: for whom will I work, and what duties will I undertake?
- ▶ Expenses: how much money will I spend, and for what items?
- ▶ Savings: how much, and in what, will I invest money?
- ▶ Sharing: how much will I give (money, time) and for what purpose?

None of these intentions are exempt from the scope of our ethical responsibilities nor is one more important than the others. The interconnectedness of these four areas applies regardless of our role—employer, employee, or consumer.

Our role in the consumer economy is an example of how tangible change must start at the individual level. While deciding how to spend or invest our money is a very important decision, it is also an opportunity. It is an opportunity to make individual choices, but also a chance to influence corporate ones. In either the role of shareholder or consumer, each individual has the opportunity to effect a change in corporate practices.

TWELVE STEPS TO CAUSING NO HARM

Skillful, compassionate choices ensure that change takes place for the better, that help is received where it is needed, and that negative consequences are avoided and positive ones promoted. Through our choices, actions, and behaviors, all grounded in positive intentions, we can all help to Create a Better Society.

> "You must be the change you wish to see in the world."
> —Mahatma Gandhi

The starting point, however, is always a leader's intentions. Leaders will have little difficulty changing the traditional paradigm—which holds that business is about profit and consumerism is the overriding good—if they believe that there is parity between people and profits. By acknowledging that alleviating suffering (regardless of its nature) is the responsibility of every person and every organization, leaders can creatively adapt their work environments into places where learning, self-development, and self-responsibility are consistently encouraged and supported.

What are the actions employers need to take to move from *unrestricted* free enterprise to a more human model of capitalism? Ideally, the end result is a corporation whose products and services create more joy in people's lives, increase the health of all sentient beings and the environment, and actively reduce problems of human suffering, such as war and poverty. By the way it does business a healthy organization would be working toward Creating a Better Society.

The following twelve steps point toward the ways in which leaders and corporations can adapt their values and behaviors to Cause No Harm while Creating Better Societies within their spheres of influence.

[1] Remind leaders and employees to be mindful of the Law of Cause and Effect. Every action has a reaction. Business decisions have consequences.

[2] Do not view the pursuit of financial viability and profit as a business' only motive. The parallel motive must be to Create a Better Society, where profitability and Causing

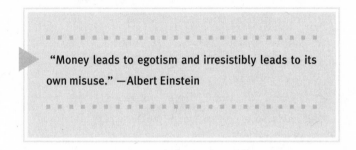

"Money leads to egotism and irresistibly leads to its own misuse." —Albert Einstein

No Harm are equally valued. Innovative solutions to make this a reality will surface when human ingenuity, good will, and the Guiding Principles are creatively and synergistically combined.

[3] Revise the direction of the business if the future vision or the current mission causes suffering.

[4] Do not manufacture and/or sell products or provide services that cause harm. To do so violates the Guiding Principle of Skillful Livelihood.

[5] Make consultation and consensus the accepted way of leading and managing the organization. Decisions based on authority or power of position have no place in the organization—they are unacceptable autocratic behaviors, stemming from the Three Poisons. Everything about the employment relationship should be open and clear for both parties to discuss and understand.

[6] Understand that our definitions of personal responsibility and corporate responsibility are one and the same.

[7] Align each and every business policy, practice, and decision with the intentions expressed in the Four Noble Truths and the Guiding Principles. (For instance, allow time and provide an appropriate space for meditation or quiet contemplation in the workplace. This would allow time during the workday for interested employees to

> Philip Morris, the world's largest tobacco company, owns Kraft Foods. So, every time people purchase Kraft brand products, they are indirectly supporting the tobacco division of the company, and hence the tobacco industry. Kraft Foods is such an integral part of Philip Morris's current effort to sanitize its public image that the parent company increased spending on corporate image advertising by 1712% between 1988 and 2000 to highlight charitable giving and their ownership of Kraft. This budget increase was for advertising—not for philanthropy or corporate giving.

focus their minds, reduce mental clutter, and work toward tranquillity.) Follow the Five Precepts as ethical touchstones.

[8] Realize that the answer to changing an unhealthy society is through non-violent behavior.

[9] View the differences between people *only* on the basis of their job performance measured against agreed-to

performance standards. This goes a long way toward freeing the corporation from all forms of violence—verbal, spiritual, psychological, physical, or sexual.

[10] Give one quarter of all profit back to society so individuals can make a better life for themselves and then assist other individuals on their journey to greater self-responsibility.

[11] Spend more time collaborating in the marketplace with your customers than competing with other manufacturers. Add value by contributing to the customer's well-being as opposed to their cravings or delusions.

[12] Cultivate the intention to create a new role for industry or trade associations (many of which are really lobby groups), namely: Creating a Better Society. They would become ethically oriented special-interest groups actively working toward the goals of Causing No Harm.

True success in business comes from living and applying the Guiding Principles and the Five Precepts in our relationships to customers, vendors, and employees. Though individuals may have

Detailed assessments of the ethical stance of major corporations are more readily available today than in the past. Many websites can educate consumers on the impact of their buying decisions. These are just a sample:

- Corp Watch (www.corpwatch.org)
- Corporate Governance (www.corpgov.net)
- Corporate Watch (www.corporatewatch.org.uk)
- Ethical Consumer (www.ethicalconsumer.org)

become attached to materialism and consumerism, out of habit or lack of understanding, this is no justification for corporations to mindlessly provide the products that feed into these behaviors.

It is fundamentally unethical to continue feeding employees and customers platitudes when they have learned (or could be taught) to think and reason for themselves. We should be innovating and providing products and services that satisfy the mind, demonstrate compassion, and offer inner peace, rather than perpetuating the production of mind-numbingly bigger, faster, and noisier products and services.

Manufacturers and consumers share a responsibility to work toward ethical and liberated states of minds. We should not be making foolish products and services for a marketplace that has not yet had the opportunity to see other, more meaningful options from the business world. Buddhist economics is about the growth of the individual, and subsequently, of society. It is time we had a look at the corporation founded under these terms.

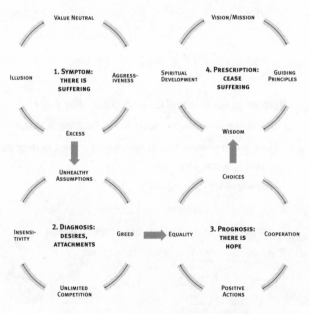

FIGURE 11.1: DOING WELL BY DOING GOOD

"From not giving to the destitute, poverty grew rife;
from poverty growing rife, stealing increased;
from the spread of stealing, violence grew apace;
from the growth of violence,
the destruction of life became common;
from the frequency of murder, the life span
and the beauty of the beings wasted away."
THE BUDDHA

12

INVITE THE BUDDHA TO YOUR BOARD MEETING: CHANGING YOUR WORLD, YOUR WORKPLACE, AND YOURSELF

FOR SOME TIME, the Honorable Lyonpo Jigmi Y Thinley, the Minister for Home Affairs in the South Asian nation of Bhutan, has been speaking out. A soft-spoken, good-humored man, his straightforward message echoes loudly. Minister Thinley captivates world audiences with his notion of Gross National Happiness (GNH). Forget traditional Western economic measures such as GNP or GDP, he argues—GNH is the best measure of a healthy society. In venues ranging from a 2003 documentary film about a soccer match between Bhutan and the Caribbean nation of Montserrat to a keynote address at the 2006 World Human Resource Congress in Singapore, Minister Thinley has articulated his vision: that we should measure the success and health of a nation by determining the emotional happiness and well-being of its populace. For me, this is a message of hope.

My intention in writing this book is to open our individual and collective eyes to the pain and suffering that is all around us, to say nothing of the pain within. My desire is to promote the value of Causing No Harm and generate a dialogue about Creating a Better Society.

I believe to my core that these things are possible.

Creating a Better Society does not mean more consumerism, it means more compassion. It does not mean more wealth for the wealthy; it means resolving, in creative ways, the overwhelming problem of poverty. Neither does it mean that the wealthy should become poorer or underprivileged; it means that our belief in the justness of "the rich becoming richer" needs to be re-examined.

My perception of reality—based on forty years of Human Resource management experience, and working with hundreds of different organizations and thousands of managers—screams at me about the imbalance between human and economic interests.

We cannot alter this imbalance, in my opinion, until we address the fact that free enterprise, in its present iteration, is a breeding ground for excess, hatred, and fundamental delusion. It does not have to be this way, but this imbalance is today's reality for many of us who live well in the developed world, just as it is for those who live in poverty. This is yet another illustration of the karmic Law of Cause and Effect, which is always present and rarely appreciated in the executive suite. But make no mistake: being unaware of the Law of Cause and Effect does not alter its impact. This is as true for individuals and corporations as it is for our society as a whole.

THE COMPASSIONATE INDIVIDUAL

The vast majority of people I meet believe that they can do very little, if anything, to Create a Better Society. But within each of us is the seed or potential to initiate and contribute to societal change. When we, as leaders or as individuals, choose anger and violence as our solutions to problems, we model this behavior (and the intentions that underlie it) to others, who view this as acceptable. But the reverse is also true; if we are compassionate and mindful, we encourage others to be the same.

Each of us carries inside us many different seeds from the karma of past and present intentions and actions which represent our potential either to do good or to not do good. Depending on how we live our lives, different seeds will grow and flourish. When we are in conflict, the seeds of anger grow and influence our thoughts and intentions. When we are calm, mindful, and at peace with ourselves—at both a physical and spiritual level—the seeds of happiness and joy flourish. On a larger scale, the more we buy into the ethos of *unrestricted* free enterprise, the more we nurture the seeds of negativity. These seeds grow into our worst capabilities.

Remember, somewhere there is a wise and compassionate doctor who has our current culture for an ailing patient. What is the symptom? Our suffering. The cause or diagnosis? Our attachments and desires for more. Yet the prognosis tells us there is hope, and part of the prescription is the addition of human values, the Eight Guiding Principles, to Western capitalism.

I have adapted the model developed by Dr. A.T. Ariyaratne of Sarvodaya to our dual goals of Causing No Harm and Creating a Better Society. The following four charts illustrate this business model.

SYMPTOM: **There Is Suffering.** This chart illustrates how value-neutral action leads to aggressiveness, which in turn leads to excess resulting in illusion. It illustrates how today's iteration of *unrestricted* capitalism leads to human suffering.

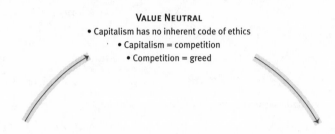

VALUE NEUTRAL
- Capitalism has no inherent code of ethics
- Capitalism = competition
- Competition = greed

ILLUSION
- Attachment to permanence = suffering
- Advertising/media = myth of consumerism
- Creating well-being with today's capitalism is an illusion

1. SYMPTOM: THERE IS SUFFERING

AGGRESSIVENESS
- Systemic need to control the marketplace
- Leadership behavior is influenced by greed, hatred, and delusions
- Put competitors out of business

EXCESS
- Unimpeded consumerism, craving for more
- Globalization vs. localization
- Excessive consumerism and spiritual development are incompatible

DIAGNOSIS: **Desires, Attachments.** This chart illustrates how our misunderstanding of permanence and unwholesome assumptions leads to attachments. Unhealthy assumptions begin a process that leads to our reinforcement of greed and its consequences of unlimited competition and insensitivity.

UNHEALTHY ASSUMPTIONS
· Corporate actions have no consequences
· There is permanence
· Greed, hatred, and
ego-gratification are
acceptable corporate realities

INSENSITIVITY
· Employees are "disposable"
· Produce anything
the customer will buy
unless legislated environmental
and health issues are imposed

**2. DIAGNOSIS:
DESIRES, ATTACHMENTS**

GREED
· Capitalism means
consumerism,
which means there
is never enough
· Leaders are obsessive about
authority/lack of trust
· Greed leads to
attachments = suffering

UNLIMITED COMPETITION
· Winning is the only value that counts
· Compete before cooperate;
fight before consensus
· Ethics, morality are obstacles

PROGNOSIS: **There Is Hope.** This chart shows the potential value of skillful choices. Here we understand that greed or excess is a choice and that attempting to hold on to the transitory is also a choice. By choosing to *Create a Better Society* we realize that co-operation with all the members of our community requires positive action and results in caring and equality.

CHOICES
· There can be a "Better Society"
· All business decisions are choices
· Apply Skillful Livelihood

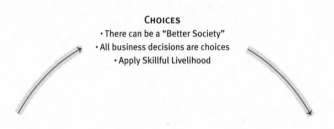

EQUALITY
· Culture could reflect positive intentions
· Relationships could reflect inter-dependence and trust
· Employees are viewed as resources, not disposable assets

3. PROGNOSIS: THERE IS HOPE

COOPERATION
· Leaders could make corporations unselfish
· Autocratic behaviors could be replaced by participative ones
· Well-being could be a priority

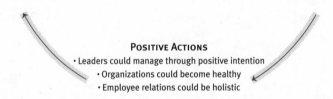

POSITIVE ACTIONS
· Leaders could manage through positive intention
· Organizations could become healthy
· Employee relations could be holistic

PRESCRIPTION: How to Cease Suffering. There is a Path out of all these kinds of human suffering. By acknowledging that capitalism is impermanent and that human well-being is, minimally, on par with profit, the Prescription is seen to be valid and we can cease suffering. We begin with skillful intentions that are articulated as a corporate vision. The Guiding Principles are the road to understanding or wisdom that leads to spiritual development—ultimately to Enlightenment—and release from the grip of suffering.

VISION/MISSION
• Profits and well-being have parity
• Create a Better Society,
be socially responsible
• Be responsible for final use
of products/services

SPIRITUAL DEVELOPMENT
• Learn to reduce attachments
• Actively contribute to the
well-being of oneself and others
• Behave in accordance
with a holistic vision

**4. PRESCRIPTION:
HOW TO CEASE
SUFFERING**

GUIDING PRINCIPLES
• Skillful intentions/actions
permeate the corporation
• Business = relationships =
integrity = Guiding Principles
• Acknowledge every business
decision has a consequence

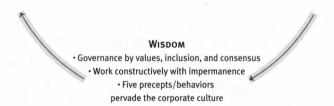

WISDOM
• Governance by values, inclusion, and consensus
• Work constructively with impermanence
• Five precepts/behaviors
pervade the corporate culture

Of course there is no neatly packageable formula on how to Create a Better Society. But Buddhism points toward a path that can lead us to the Middle Way—and I hope I have helped you to appreciate that path. I enthusiastically encourage all of us to take the first steps along that path, to grab hold of our hopes and potential for adaptation, and actively engage in helping our society change and grow. As you prepare to take the first step on that journey, here are some principles to keep in mind:

> Work toward self-reliance (a core ingredient in happiness) and away from the insidious domination of consumerism.

> Hold all levels of government to higher ethical and spiritual standards.

> Strive to become a community leader who works for a better society.

Traditionally, Buddhism places a strong emphasis on overcoming poverty. Poverty is a major hindrance (if not *the* major hindrance) to our ability to actualize self-reliance, and poverty is a primary initiator of hatred, crime, and even war. Economic self-sufficiency is a prerequisite for a stable community. This, in turn, lays the foundation that enables individuals and groups to follow the Eight Guiding Principles.

THE GLOBAL COMMUNITY: CREATING A BETTER SOCIETY

I have emphasized that the journey toward what Buddhists would consider awareness and liberation must begin with the individual. Yet the preceding discussion of poverty as a hindrance to living the Eight Guiding Principles makes clear that there are large global or societal issues at play which can render the journey harder or easier, an unsurprising conclusion in an interconnected world. It is important to recognize these issues and what we must do to address them, but we must also not lose sight of the fact that only the self-responsible individual can begin to effect change with others.

Once we are prepared to engage these concerns, there are a number of issues on which to focus. I offer the following recommendations as a starting point—for both debate and action—for Creating a Better Society.

▶ *We need a global response to globalization.* Our political, social, legal, and judicial systems have not kept pace with the rapid changes in the global marketplace. The legal framework for transnationals that operate outside their own boundaries is not well established, and nor is the legal framework for small, indigenous businesses that compete in their own countries with these transnationals well established. Developing nations need to establish their own strategies, tactics, and rules so that they can negotiate more effectively with developed countries.

▶ *Conflict resolution within and between societies must be based on our natural human interdependence.* War should become a thing of the past. A better society will emerge when the global military industry is seen as a cause rather than the deterrent to suffering.

▶ *We must work to end the fascination with consumerism, which leads to hatred and delusion.* The need is to respond with information and education so that emphasis is placed on creating self-reliant communities where consumerism and materialism are seen for what they truly are: myths of happiness.

▶ *If people are to learn to be responsible for their intentions and actions, the societies within which they live (including their political and legal systems) must be decentralized, egalitarian, and democratic.* Today, more power is wielded by corporate boardrooms than it is by the halls of government. So the boardroom must understand and respect this responsibility to be decentralized, egalitarian, and democratic. Too often, however, the *unrestricted* free enterprise speaks to authority, power, and greed.

▶ *The Four Noble Truths are a blueprint to Creating a Better Society.* This is true in at least three ways. First, following the Four Noble Truths would allow people to live their lives without the fear of poverty, disease, and famine. When faced with these insecurities, people become deeply embedded in their own suffering. Second, people would be able to live their lives free from both discrimination in all its forms and arbitrary governmental intervention without domestic debate and consensus. Wisdom, tolerance, compassion, benevolence, and access to education would be hallmarks of our communities. Finally, people would be able to achieve personal freedom, whether that is through the creative use of their talents or through a spiritual quest. In living by the Four Noble Truths, people would experience the Buddha's prescription: identify their suffering, understand the chains of craving, learn that detachment is within their grasp, and finally live family, work, and spiritual lives that follow the Middle Way.

HOW BUDDHISM CAN INFLUENCE CAPITALISM

Following are several illustrations of capitalism today, and an example of what the Buddhist influence on them would be.

▶ *Capitalism today:* Capital or business financing is obtained through one's own wealth, venture capital, or more tradition- ally by selling partial ownership of the business (stocks, bonds, and other financial instruments). From this capital, a legal entity—a corporation—is granted a charter by the government to conduct business.

Buddhist influence: The requirements for receiving a corpo- rate charter would be expanded to include responsibility for Causing No Harm and a focus on Creating a Better Society. A renewal process would accompany each corporate char- ter. Charters would not be granted with an indefinite time- line and no accountability to Cause No Harm.

▶ *Capitalism today:* Those with entrepreneurial skills use the capital they have acquired to create new and innovative products and services for the marketplace.

Buddhist influence: It would be ensured that these products and service Cause No Harm to individuals, communities, and the environment.

▶ *Capitalism today:* Workplaces are created to facilitate the design, manufacture, and distribution of consumer goods for the purposes of creating wealth.

Buddhist influence: It would be ensured that ethical values that support the well-being of individuals and society are the benchmark against which all commercial activities are measured.

▶ *Capitalism today:* Advertising and marketing of products lead to sales revenue that supports operating expenses and provides profit. This marketing and selling of products adopts the mantra, "more is better." The corporation has no obligation or responsibility as to how its products are used. The buyer must beware.

Buddhist influence: Corporations would be required to be responsible for the products they manufacture, for the safe (non-harmful) use of these products, and for leaving the environment as healthy as they found it. The principle of Causing No Harm would apply equally to producer and user.

Among the wealthiest countries, the economically developed countries of the "G8," poverty is still alarmingly high. According to the 2004 Human Development Report (independent data commissioned annually by the United Nations), poverty, as a percentage of population, in these countries is:

- USA—17.0%
- Canada—12.8%
- Italy—12.7%
- Great Britain—12.5%

- Japan—11.8%
- Germany—8.3%
- France—8.0%
- Russian Federation—no data

▶ *Capitalism today:* Payroll is a business expense. It reduces profits. There is a direct relationship between "high value for payroll dollars" and profitability.

Buddhist influence: Employers would have an inherent responsibility to support the well-being of employees, to recognize that people have value. A similar responsibility would exist for employees toward employers.

▶ *Capitalism today*: Profits can be taken out of the business (e.g., bonuses to owners, dividends to stockholders, etc.), reinvested in new product research and development, or used to update existing products or technologies.

Buddhist influence: It would be ensured that profitability reflects both financial success and human well-being. Any calculation to determine the worth of a corporation's stock would include a percentage assigned to financial success and a percentage to employee or community development. If the intentions were there, the difference would show up in our communities and around the globe as increased human well-being, reduced poverty, and an improved society.

▶ *Capitalism today*: The goal is to sell more of our products/services than our competitors and obtain the largest possible market share with the greatest profit margins.

Buddhist influence: Greater emphasis would be placed on collaboration rather than competition and its win-lose consequences. The economic system would reward partnering, joint ventures, etc., that demonstrate a benefit to society.

▶ *Capitalism today*: In order to influence the buyer's choice, life-style advertising, public relations, philanthropy, etc., are used to highlight corporations and/or their brands.

Buddhist influence: The collaboration of corporations, communities, and governments to develop and implement standards for ethical advertising would be encouraged. The goal is to Cause No Harm and, while doing so, continuously improve the well-being of communities.

▶ *Capitalism today:* Lobby groups are established to influence legislators and funds are made available to pro-business candidates running for political office to protect corporate interests, in issues ranging from employment legislation to environmental health and safety regulations.

Buddhist influence: Abstention from additional restrictions or governmental intervention would be encouraged, but *only* if businesses have adopted the Middle Way suggested by the earlier steps. By applying the Cause No Harm value, the *unrestricted* nature of free enterprise will diminish.

▶ *Capitalism today:* Free enterprise generally has no size or geographic limitations, so it is a natural extension of the business to move into other marketplaces around the world. Laws and regulations in the corporation's home country rarely apply in other parts of the world.

Buddhist influence: The harmful impact of globalization would be addressed by including human values in a new iteration of capitalism. While efforts to ensure that the laws of its home country govern a corporation's activities elsewhere are important, following the previous steps goes a long way toward mitigating the need for such regulation.

A "Better Society" is manifest in the following seven domains:

- *Philosophy*: Consistent with the Four Noble Truths, the focus is on enhancing the quality of life rather than on consumerism and materialism—that is, focusing on being rather than having. The Eight Guiding Principles become our touchstones.

- *Values:* Based on the principle of reverence for all sentient beings, compassion and non-violence promote harmony within and between societies as well as with the natural world.

- *Individuals:* Self-awareness and self-responsibility are hallmarks. The practices of Skillful Concentration and Skillful Mindfulness are encouraged and supported.

- *Economy:* Cooperative rather than competitive practices change the direction of free enterprise. This would include a redistribution of wealth so that all members of the society enjoy a supportive and healthy standard of living.

- *Resources:* Used relative to availability and sustainability. By mutual consent, the manufacturing of goods is limited to satisfying the society's fundamental needs and requirements. To aid in supporting a society based on the desire of "non-suffering," goods and services are viewed not only from the perspective of need but also from their ability to become attachments.

- *Environment:* Society would practice a holistic stewardship over nature, so that human activities would have limited environmental impact.

- *Population:* Size based on the availability of renewable natural and human resources; diversity based on a society's ability to include varied ethnic communities.

CONCLUSION

Mine is not a cry for revolution but for the direct integration of human values into our economic system. This can only happen in an evolutionary manner, so we need to better understand the interdependent cause-and-effect relationships between economics and human suffering. Then we need to determine our priorities: people before profits, profits before people, or parity between the two? By refocusing our intentions, capitalism can evolve into a system that incorporates human values without losing the benefits of a free-market economy.

AFTERWORD

FROM A PRESENTATION MADE AT A "SPIRITUALITY IN THE WORKPLACE" CONFERENCE, TORONTO METRO CENTRE, BY LLOYD M. FIELD

AT THE CORE OF MY THESIS is the view that the business community has the yet-to-be-tapped capacity to change—for the better—the world we have created for ourselves.

The game plan that tallies the successes and failures for business is derived from our current notion of free enterprise. By its very nature free enterprise prefers freedom from as many restrictions (legislation, regulations, etc.) as society might possibly impose. Why have constraints on the road to success? And success has but one universal definition: ever-increasing return on investment (ROI). No business enterprise receives accolades for conducting its affairs with compassion and wisdom as its *raison d'etre*. Such characteristics have no place in a world directed at globalization, materialism, shareholders' needs for maximum return—and instead, focus is on increasing the profitable bottom line. Indeed, it is not in our capitalist vocabulary to say we made too much profit—and even too much is never enough! But it is the absence from free enterprise of the compassion and the wisdom of our spiritual traditions that has led to this *greed of excess* and its negative consequences—human, environmental, societal, and otherwise.

By clinging to an illusion of permanence and the view that money is the "real" solution, we misunderstand the suffering of all those around us. Truly they are us and we are them!

So: Can free enterprise make a positive difference? Can business approach the reduction of poverty with the same vision and rigor that it uses to gain greater market share? I believe it can!

The key to seeing this happen is to move free enterprise or capitalism to its next iteration, by creating a system whereby the *index of success* is a *blended calculation* representing ROI (in much the same manner as we calculate it now) and a scorecard for Causing No Harm and Creating a Better Society. Together, we need to create this index. Some stock exchanges—such as the London Stock Exchange—are already working with similar ideas.

If we implement these ideas, a corporation would engage in such activities as Causing No Harm and Creating a Better Society because that would be part of the "new rules" of *how we do capitalism.* Success would be indicated by the combination of leading a profitable enterprise, Causing No Harm to any sentient being and the environment, and contributing to the enhancement of our communities. With everyone using the same rules, no one is at a disadvantage.

The ideal of reducing human suffering is at the core of every faith tradition—it is not a new idea. But compassion and the present iteration of capitalism do not mix well—and so we must change the rules so that the *greed of excess* is no longer valued as a positive attribute or a measure of success. This is not an issue of philanthropy or Corporate Social Responsibility; this is a sea-change to a new system in which the notions of a business's success and of that business's doing good are inextricably connected!

My goal is to initiate a dialogue about the ways and means of including human values in our definition and practices of capitalism. Since we get what we value, let's value human well being first and foremost!

APPENDIX I:
SUMMARY OF SUGGESTIONS FOR INITIATING
POSITIVE CHANGES WITHIN OUR ORGANIZATIONS

STRATEGIC PLANNING

▶ The Eight Guiding Principles and the Ethical Code (Five Precepts) will be our guide.

▶ We will not accept or initiate any business activities that violate the Guiding Principle of Skillful Livelihood.

▶ To ensure positive outcomes, we will spend time on consensus building and understanding the strategic direction and intentions of the business.

▶ The business' Value and Mission statements will be driven by a belief that Creating a Better Society and earning a *reasonable* return on investment are valued by the organization.

HUMAN RESOURCES

▶ Nothing is more important to our organization than the people it employs. We will respect and engage them accordingly.

▶ Our leaders must model the Guiding Principles and the Ethical Code in all their intentions, decisions, and actions.

▶ We will ensure that every employee understands how his/her position and role can positively impact the dual goals of Creating a Better Society and profitability.

▶ Our employees, after appropriate introspection, investigation, discussion, and agreement will undertake to conduct *all* their relationships by using the Guiding Principles and the Ethical Code.

▶ In all business interactions, people will be coached in how to accept more self-responsibility and accountability.

▶ In developing and implementing Human Resource policies and practices, we will act as though applicable legislation is the lowest common denominator.

▶ Every workplace will have a quiet space for personal self-development (e.g., meditation, prayer, personal reflection, etc.).

MARKETING, SALES, ADVERTISING, PUBLIC RELATIONS

▶ We will be guided by honest, transparent communications with all stakeholders. Skillful Speech will be our guide.

▶ We will communicate with integrity about products and services that ensure the consumer's non-suffering and lack of attachment.

▶ The ways in which the organization's products/services contribute to Creating a Better Society will always be visible.

▶ These approaches to public communications will highlight the fact that our commitment to being profitable while Creating a Better Society demonstrates our integrity.

MANUFACTURING

▶ The physical and emotional well-being of people comes first; production targets and customer deadlines come second.

▶ We will not use methods, processes, or components that, in the final product, will cause harm to others.

▶ We will only create products/services that add to the well-being of people.

▶ We will work to rejuvenate the environment and protect ecosystems.

FINANCE

▶ Financial transparency will be our watchword.

▶ Financial success and employee/customer well-being will have parity.

▶ We will meet all commitments to stakeholders (e.g., warranties, dividends, payroll).

▶ Unethical or illegal transactions will not be tolerated.

▶ We will not make significant financial decisions that would impact the lives of the employees and other stakeholders without their consensus (e.g., pension plan changes).

▶ Tax-avoidance measures that would result in causing harm to the greater community will not be tolerated.

▶ We will not knowingly participate in illegal, unethical, or immoral transactions.

APPENDIX II:
EXERCISES FOR INDIVIDUAL INQUIRY

▶ Do you agree with the Buddhist principle that everything (from thoughts to "things") is impermanent? What are your reasons for your answer? What implications does this principle of impermanence have for you as a business leader or as a consumer?

▶ If you think of your career or job as routine or even drudgery—but you are in no position to leave your employment—how do you presently deal with this "suffering"? Considering Buddha's message (about suffering and the alleviation of suffering), what other options might be open to you?

▶ Does your organization have a social responsibility beyond maximizing profits? What are the reasons for your answer? What are the implications of your answer to yourself, your community, and your business?

▶ Is profit the goal of business or the measure of how well one conducts one's business affairs? What intentions are at the core of your answer?

▶ As a business leader, do you believe that survival of your business is so important that you would violate your own integrity—that is, create suffering for others—to keep your business going?

▶ Focus, for a moment, on all the possessions that you own. After thinking about these objects for a few moments, bring your mind to a crisis that you have experienced—death of a parent or a child, grave illness, a serious car accident, etc. How much value or importance did these favorite possessions have during such a crisis? Can you draw the conclusion that during periods of crisis all material objects had very little importance? What therefore is the true value of consumerism for you?

▶ The Buddha would have argued that unfettered or unrestricted free enterprise is harmful to society—it is not the Middle Way. What is your opinion about this statement? What suggestions do you have to reduce the consequences, and to increase the positive outcomes, of today's iteration of capitalism?

▶ As a private shareholder, would you be willing to take less dividend income if it meant corporations conducted themselves so that they Caused No Harm? What are the motivations behind your answer?

▶ As you look at your colleagues, you will likely see a tendency to be "business people" during the week and "family people" on the weekends. Do you believe that people can separate their lives in such a manner? If so, how would you argue that an individual could have different core values—those at work and those at home? If not, describe how people apply themselves holistically to everything they do.

▶ How would you help implement in your organization the Core Value of Causing No Harm and Creating a Better Society?

▶ To what degree does *how* a corporation earns its profits matter? Is compliance with the law sufficient for a corporation to say it has fulfilled its ethical and moral responsibilities?

▶ The United States is presently the world's largest developer, manufacturer, and marketer of military weapons. What are the advantages and disadvantages of being in such a position? Does this position conflict with the espoused democratic and social values of the United States?

▶ The United States came into being because its citizens revolted against excessive government and corporate power. The Boston Tea Party and the ensuing Colonial War was a reaction to a British Crown corporation with monopoly powers. Given the present commercial influence of the American economy on the global markets, what have the people behind the Western globalization movement learned from this history? In what ways are current-day rebellions, terrorism, and wars provoked by the power of transnationals? Where does militant fundamentalism or terrorism fit into this picture?

▶ There is clear evidence that a few hundred transnational corporations dominate world trade, and a handful of mega-corporations control the world's media. An even smaller number of first-rate research centers determine the world's scientific and technological agenda. The leaders of these organizations have powers greater than most governments.

These realities currently underpin the present global economy. How have you and your family benefited and/or suffered as a result of globalization? How has society (both in the developed and developing worlds) benefited and/or suffered as a result of globalization?

▶ To ensure that customers continue to purchase products and services, massive amounts of corporate money are spent on advertising. The consumer gets "hooked" on the idea that material possessions create happiness or that they lead to non-suffering. Can a corporation's advertising message (in regards to this type of illusion) be changed? If so, how? If not, why?

▶ Does the job or the role that you perform contain any components or aspects that cause harm or injury to others? Describe the harm that is caused. What options are open to you to alter your job or your corporation, so that no harm is caused?

▶ By altering our mindset so that we are fully present and knowledgeable about what it is that we are doing (moment-by-moment mindfulness), we become aware of our intentions and can therefore make choices about what we do. How might your company alter its paradigm so that its intentions are clear for everyone to see and discuss? Would such a paradigm change be a positive move?

▶ How might the positive intentions, inherent in the Eight Guiding Principles, be applied to your organization? Record the actions to be taken and develop an initial timeline for implementation.

THE PRACTICE: MINDFULNESS OF BREATHING WITH RELAXATION

FROM *THE ATTENTION REVOLUTION* BY B. ALAN WALLACE

Our minds are bound up with our bodies, so we need to incorporate our bodies into meditative practice. In each session we will do this by first settling the body in its natural state, while imbued with three qualities: relaxation, stillness, and vigilance.

THE POSTURE

It is generally preferable to practice meditation sitting on a cushion with your legs crossed. But if that is uncomfortable, you may either sit on a chair or lie down in the supine position (on your back), your head resting on a pillow. Whatever position you assume, let your back be straight, and settle your body with a sense of relaxation and ease. Your eyes may be closed, hooded (partially closed), or open, as you wish. My own preference when practicing mindfulness of breathing is to close my eyes partially, with just a little light coming in, and I like to meditate in a softly lit room. Wear loose, comfortable clothing that doesn't restrict your waist or abdomen.

If you are sitting, you may rest your hands on your knees or in your lap. Your head may be slightly inclined or directed straight ahead, and your tongue may lightly touch your palate. Now bring your awareness to the tactile sensations throughout your body, from the soles of your feet up to the crown of your head. Note the sensations in your shoulders and neck, and if you detect any tightness there, release it. Likewise, be aware of the muscles of your face—your jaws, temples, and forehead, as well as your eyes—and soften any area that feels constricted. Let your face relax like that of a sleeping baby, and set your entire body at ease.

Throughout this session, keep as physically still as you can. Avoid all unnecessary movement, such as scratching and fidgeting. You will find that the stillness of the body helps to settle the mind.

If you are sitting, assume a "posture of vigilance": Slightly raise your sternum so that when you inhale, you feel the sensations of the respiration naturally go to your belly, which expands during the in-breath and retracts during the out-breath. During meditation sessions, breathe as if you were pouring water into a pot, filling it from the bottom up. When the breath is shallow, only the belly will expand. In the course of a deeper inhalation, first the abdomen, then the diaphragm will then expand, and when you inhale yet more deeply, the chest will finally expand after the belly and diaphragm have done so.

If you are meditating in the supine position, position yourself so that you can mentally draw a straight line from the point between your heels, to your navel, and to your chin. Let your feet fall to the outside, and stretch your arms out about thirty degrees from your torso, with your palms facing up. Rest your head on a pillow. You may find it helpful to place a cushion under your knees to help relax the back. Vigilance in the supine position is mostly psychological, an attitude that regards this position as a formal meditation posture, and not simply as rest.

THE PRACTICE

Be at ease. Be still. Be vigilant. These three qualities of the body are to be maintained throughout all meditation sessions. Once you have settled your body with these three qualities, take three slow, gentle, deep breaths, breathing in and out through the nostrils. Let your awareness permeate your entire body as you do so, noting any sensations that arise in relation to the respiration. Luxuriate in these breaths, as if you were receiving a gentle massage from within.

Now settle your respiration in its natural flow. Continue breathing through your nostrils, noting the sensations of the respiration wherever they arise within your body. Observe the entire course of each in- and out-breath, noting whether it is long or short, deep or shallow, slow or fast. Don't impose any rhythm on your breathing. Attend closely to the respiration, but without willfully influencing it in any way. Don't even prefer one kind of a breath over another, and don't assume that rhythmic breathing is necessarily better than irregular breathing. Let the body breathe as if you were fast asleep, but mindfully vigilant.

Thoughts are bound to arise involuntarily, and your attention may also be pulled away by noises and other stimuli from your environment. When you note that you have become distracted, instead of tightening up and forcing your attention back to the breath, simply let go of these thoughts and distractions. Especially with each out-breath, relax your body, release extraneous thoughts, and happily let your attention settle back into the body. When you see that your mind has wandered, don't get upset. Just be happy that you've noticed the distraction, and gently return to the breath.

Again and again, counteract the agitation and turbulence of the mind by relaxing more deeply, not by contracting your body or mind. If any tension builds up in your shoulders, face, or eyes, release it. With each exhalation, release involuntary thoughts as if they were dry leaves blown away by a soft breeze. Relax deeply through the entire course of the exhalation, and continue to relax as the next breath flows in effortlessly like the tide. Breathe so effortlessly that you feel as if your body were being breathed by your environment.

Continue practicing for one twenty-four-minute period, then mindfully emerge from meditation and reengage with the world around you.

GLOSSARY OF BUDDHIST TERMS

Bodhisattva One who renounces entry into *nirvana* until all beings
have been taught and similarly worked their way along the path. A
bodhisattva demonstrates utmost compassion and wisdom by fore-
stalling his/her entry into *nirvana* so as to be of assistance to others.

Buddha A fully enlightened being; one who has "woken up" completely, and is living a life fully supported by compassion, ethics,
and wisdom. "The Buddha" often refers to Siddhartha Gautama,
the historical Buddha who lived in India around 2,500 years ago.

Dharma The teachings of the historical Buddha, or Buddhist teachings. Also refers to the phenomenal universe itself.

Dukkha Suffering in all its forms (e.g. birth, illness, disassociation from
loved ones, not getting what one wants, greed, death).

Enlightenment A way of expressing the "awakening" of a being from
suffering. It is the non-realization or non-understanding of emptiness
and impermanence that keeps all beings attached to suffering. Upon
enlightenment, a being fully understands these things.

Five Hindrances States of mind that block one's innate wholesome
qualities (e.g. compassion, ethical behavior, wisdom). These hindrances negatively override the process of meditation as one works
toward awakening. They are: (1) a desire for pleasures from any of
our senses (in Buddhism the mind is considered one of the six
senses); (2) ill-will toward other sentient beings or a subjective

form of aversion to what is wholesome in one's being; (3) lethargy or dullness; (4) worry, restlessness, or being in a state of unease; (5) vacillation or fearfulness. These five hindrances are, in one form or another, aspects of greed, hatred, and delusion about reality. They are obstacles to positive intentions and skillful behaviors (including meditation).

Five Precepts A code of conduct with the express purpose of protecting one from unwholesome and unskillful intentions, thoughts, and behaviors. They are the commitments to: (1) abstain from harming or destroying living beings. By acting with *loving-kindness* and out of compassion one can control the passion of hate and anger which, if left unchecked, would lead to harming others. (2) Abstain from taking what is not given. By acting with generosity and sincerity, one is demonstrating trustworthiness and thus avoiding taking from others. (3) Abstain from sensual misconduct such as adultery. By curbing lust (in any of its forms) we cultivate contentment and show respect for and behave with integrity toward others. (4) Abstain from false speech such as lying, deceiving, gossiping, or any similar unwholesome behaviors. By not cheating, exaggerating, or slandering, etc., we demonstrate our honesty and integrity. (5) Abstain from drugs, alcohol, or any intoxicants that cloud one's senses (such as causing an inability to be mindful or even meditate) or act as an escapism from reality. By being mindful, one can understand reality and demonstrate self-control over one's intentions, thoughts, and behaviors.

Four Noble Truths The basis for all Buddhist teachings. Using a medical analogy, the First Truth is the symptom: there is suffering. The Second Truth is the diagnosis: our desires and attachments cause suffering. The Third Truth is the prognosis: a cure does exist. The Fourth Truth is the prescription: follow the path that leads away from suffering, namely the Eightfold Path.

Karma Literally, "action"; the cosmic law of cause and effect. All actions fall into one of three categories: mental, verbal, and physical. It is the intention behind the action that is karma. Karma can be positive and wholesome or it can be negative and unwholesome. The seeds of wholesome actions obtain fruition in wholesome effects and consequences; the seeds of unwholesome actions obtain fruition in unwholesome effects and consequences.

Metta **or Loving-kindness** A concern for the well-being and happiness of oneself and others. It can also be viewed as the positive intentions and behaviors that overcome fear, anger/hatred, and greed. Metta is related to the Guiding Principle of Skillful Thought and manifests itself as generosity.

The Middle Way The path that avoids the two extremes of ascetic renunciation and of pleasure-seeking and other efforts to gratify one's endless desires.

Noble Eightfold Path The Path is the Fourth Noble Truth, which leads to a release from suffering. The *Eightfold Path,* or the Eight Guiding Principles (as referred to in this book), is related to positive or non-harmful intentions and skillful or wise ways of implementing these Principles. The Eight Principles and their insightful application make up what is referred to as Buddhism.

Samadhi Single-pointedness of concentration. It is referred to in the Guiding Principle of Concentration.

Samsara The continuous cycle of birth and rebirth into suffering. To leave the cycle of samsara one must understand the Four Noble Truths and walk the Eightfold Path; that is, one must create positive karma in all of one's intentions. To have broken free of this cycle of suffering (birth and rebirth) is to have attained liberation, or enlightenment.

Vipassana Insight meditation. A deep meditation that exposes the truth about impermanence, suffering, and egolessness. Insight is not the result of a mere intellectual understanding but is achieved through direct meditative observation.

FURTHER READING

Ariyaratne, A.T. *Buddhist Economics in Practice*. Salisbury, U.K.: Sarvodaya Support Group, 1999.

Attenborough, Richard. *The Words of Gandhi*. New York: Newmarket Press, 1982.

Autry, James and Stephen Mitchell. *Real Power: Business Lessons from the Tao Te Ching*. New York: Riverhead Books, 1999.

Barber, Benjamin. *Jihad vs. McWorld*. New York: Ballantine Books, 1996.

Bodhi, Bhikkhu. *Noble Eightfold Path, Way to the End of Suffering*. Kandy, Sri Lanka: Buddhist Publication Society, 1984.

———. *Middle Length Discourses of the Buddha*. Boston: Wisdom Publications, 1995.

———. *Connected Discourses of the Buddha*. Boston: Wisdom Publications, 2000.

Boritharvwanaket, K.S. *Metta: Lovingkindness in Buddhism*. London: Triple Gem Press, 1995.

Brandt, Barbara. *Whole Life Economics*. Gabriola Island, BC, Canada: New Society Publishers, 1995.

Capra, Fritjof. *The Turning Point*. New York: Simon & Schuster, 1982.

Chakraborty, S.K. *Management by Values: Toward Cultural Congruence*. New Delhi, India: Oxford University Press, 1992.

Chappel, David W., Editor. *Buddhist Peacework: Creating Cultures of Peace*. Boston: Wisdom Publications, 1999.

Cheetham, Eric. *Fundamentals of Mainstream Buddhism*. Boston: Tuttle Company, 1994.

Cleary, Thomas. *Book of Leadership & Strategy: Lessons of the Chinese Masters*. Boston: Shambhala Publications, 1992.

Damma, Rewata. *First Discourse of the Buddha*. Boston: Wisdom Publications, 1997.

Field, Lloyd. *Unions Are Not Inevitable!* 4th ed. Waterloo, ON, Canada: Brock Learning Resources, 2001.

Fitz-enz, Jac. *ROI of Human Capital: Measuring the Economic Value of Employee Performance*. New York: AMACOM, 2000.

Fox, Mathew. *Reinvention of Work: A New Vision of Livelihood for Our Time*. New York: Harper Collins Publishers, 1994.

Gold, Tara. *Open Your Mind, Open Your Life*. Kansas City: Lionstead Press, 2002.

Goldstein, Joseph and Jack Kornfield. *Seeking the Heart of Wisdom*. Boston: Shambhala Publications, 1987.

Gunaratana, Bhante Henepola. *Eight Mindful Steps to Happiness*. Boston: Wisdom Publications, 2001.

———. *Mindfulness in Plain English*. Boston: Wisdom Publications, 1994.

Hahn, Thich Nhat. *Heart of the Buddha's Teaching*. Berkeley, CA: Parallax Press, 1998.

———. *Interbeing*. Berkeley, CA: Parallax Press, 1998.

Harvey, Peter. *Introduction to Buddhism*. Cambridge, U.K.: Cambridge University Press, 1990.

———. *Introduction to Buddhist Ethics*. Cambridge, U.K.: Cambridge University Press, 2000.

Hawkens, P. and H. Lovins. *Natural Capitalism.* New York: Harper Collins, 1994.

Hawkens, Paul. *Growing a Business.* New York: Harper Collins, 1998.

Hawley, Jack. *Reawakening the Spirit in Work.* New York: Fireside/Simon & Schuster, 1993.

Herman, Stanley M. *Tao at Work: On Leading and Following.* San Francisco: Jossey-Bass Publishers, 1994.

Hershock, Peter. *Reinventing the Wheel: A Buddhist Response to the Information Age.* Albany, NY: State University of New York Press, 1999.

Houlder, Dominic. *Mindfulness and Money.* New York: Broadway Books, 2002.

Inoue, Shinichi. *Putting Buddhism to Work.* New York: Kodansha International, 1997.

Kabat-Zinn, Jon. *Wherever You Go There You Are.* New York: Hyperion, 1994.

Kaza, S. and K. Kraft, Editors. *Dharma Rain.* Boston: Shambhala Publications, 2000.

Keynes, John M. *General Theory of Employment: Interest and Money.* London: MacMillan Publishers, 1939.

Kohr, Leopold. *Breakdown of Nations (The).* London: Kegan and Paul Publishers, 1957.

Kornfield, Jack. *A Path With Heart.* New York: Random House, 1993.

Larkin, Geri. *Building a Business the Buddhist Way.* Berkeley, CA: Celestial Arts, 1999.

Macy, Joanna. *Dharma and Development.* West Hartford, CT: Kumarian Press, 1991.

———. *Mutual Causality in Buddhism and General Systems Theory.* Albany, NY: State University of New York Press, 1991.

Macy, Joanna and Molly Young. *Coming Back to Life: Practices to Reconnect Our Lives, Our World.* Gabriola Island, BC, Canada: New Society Publishers, 1998.

Maslow, A.H. *Maslow on Management.* New York: John Wiley & Sons, 1998.

———. *Understanding Human Motivation.* Cleveland: H. Allen Publishers, 1958.

Mori, Masahiro. *The Buddha in the Robot.* Tokyo: Kosei Publishing Co., 1985.

Narada. *Buddha and His Teachings.* Taipei, Taiwan: Buddha Education Foundation, 1997.

Payutto, Bhikkhu. *Buddhist Economics.* Bangkok: Buddhadamma Foundation Publications, 1992.

Radhakrishnan, S., Editor. *Dhammapada.* Delhi: Oxford India Paperbacks, Oxford University Press, 1997.

Reichold, Frederick. *Loyalty Effect: The Hidden Force behind Growth, Profits, and Lasting Value.* Boston: Harvard Business School Press, 1996.

Richmond, Lewis. *Work as a Spiritual Practice.* New York: Broadway Books, 1999.

Rosen, Robert. *Healthy Company.* Los Angeles: Jeremy P. Tarcher Publishers, 1991.

Rosenberg, Larry. *Breath by Breath.* Boston: Shambhala Publications, 1998.

Rowland, Wade. *How Corporations Rule the World and How We Let It Happen.* Toronto: Thomas Allen Publishers, 2005.

Rinpoche, Sogyal. *The Tibetan Book of Living and Dying.* San Francisco: Harper Collins, 1992.

Saddhatissa, Hammalawa. *Buddhist Ethics.* Boston: Wisdom Publications, 1997.

Salzberg, Sharon. *Loving-kindness: The Revolutionary Art of Happiness.* Boston: Shambhala Press, 1997.

Schumacher, E.F. *Small Is Beautiful: Economics as if People Mattered.* New York: Harper Collins, 1973.

Settel, Trudy. *Book of Gandhi Wisdom.* Secaucus, NJ: Carol Publishing, 1997.

Sivaraksa, Sulak. *Seeds of Peace: A Buddhist Vision for Renewing Society.* Berkeley, CA: Parallex Press, 1992.

Smith, Adam. *Theory of Moral Sentiments.* Buffalo, NY: Prometheus Books, 2001.

———. *Wealth of Nations.* New York: Bantam Books, 2003.

Thurman, Robert. *Inner Revolution.* New York: Riverhead Books, 1998.

Toynbee, A.J. *Study of History.* Oxford, U.K.: Oxford University Press, 1987.

Tucker. M.E. and D.R. Williams, Editors. *Buddhism and Ecology.* Boston: Harvard University Press, 1997.

Walshe, Maurice, Editor. *Long Discourses of the Buddha.* Boston: Wisdom Publications, 1995.

Warder, A.K. *Indian Buddhism.* 3rd ed. Delhi: Motilal Banarsidass Press, 2000.

Wimala, Bhante Y. *Lessons of the Lotus.* New York: Bantam Books, 1997.

ACKNOWLEDGMENTS

The generosity that family, friends, and colleagues have shown me throughout this lengthy project can only be described as overwhelming. Everyone I talked with provided sound advice and critical observations. If this book meets its objective of opening a dialogue on the nature of capitalism and its potential impact to improve human well-being, it will be in great part because of the generous support of many people.

My efforts would not have seen the light of day if not for the writing and editorial support of Lauren Nesbitt and my son, Russell.

Research advice and peer review were provided by Paul Born, M.A., Laszlo Bodnar, Ph.D., Richard Brooks, Otto Chang, Ph.D., Ari Dassanayake, Ph.D., Wayne Fisher, M.A., Thupten Jinpa, Ph.D., Upali Kuruppu, Ph.D., Michael Koo, Ph.D., Ron Knowles, M.B.A., Tilosewa Pelpola, L.L.B., Venerable Madawela Punnaji, and Venerable Shish Miao Hsin.

During the dark days of depression, support and clarity came from many people—notably from my wife Joyce, our son Russell, Lauren Nesbitt, and two special friends: Cheryl Leis, Ph.D., and Ron Pond, M.D.

My appreciation goes to the staff at Wisdom, especially to Josh Bartok and Gustavo Szpilman Cutz for their assistance with the final editing, to Rod Meade Sperry for his efforts in the promotion of this book, and Tony Lulek for production of this book.

I am forever humbled by the encouragement and endorsements provided by H.H. the Dalai Lama, Venerable Master Hsing Yun, and Dr. A.T. Ariyaratne.

INDEX

ABOUT THE AUTHOR

LLOYD FIELD PH.D., left his position as a corporate Vice President of Human Resources at Johnson & Johnson International to build a new career in Organizational Development and Human Resource consultancy. His clients have included many Fortune 500 organizations and his management development and training audiences have included more than 20,000 managers in North America, Europe, and Asia. His current focus is on helping senior executives solve business problems through Buddhist-influenced coaching and counseling. A classic connector in the Malcolm Gladwell sense of the word, Lloyd has sold over 10,000 copies (in Canada) of his previous book on positive employee relations—that book is soon to be in its fifth edition. You can contact Lloyd through his website at www.lloydfield.com.

About Wisdom Publications

WISDOM **PUBLICATIONS,** a nonprofit publisher, is dedicated to making available authentic works relating to Buddhism for the benefit of all. We publish books by ancient and modern masters in all traditions of Buddhism, translations of important texts, and original scholarship. Additionally, we offer books that explore East-West themes unfolding as traditional Buddhism encounters our modern culture in all its aspects. Our titles are published with the appreciation of Buddhism as a living philosophy, and with the special commitment to preserve and transmit important works from Buddhism's many traditions.

To learn more about Wisdom, or to browse books online, visit our website at www.wisdompubs.org.

You may request a copy of our catalog online or by writing to this address:

Wisdom Publications
199 Elm Street
Somerville, Massachusetts 02144 USA
Telephone: 617-776-7416 • Fax: 617-776-7841
Email: info@wisdompubs.org • www.wisdompubs.org

THE WISDOM TRUST

As a nonprofit publisher, Wisdom is dedicated to the publication of Dharma books for the benefit of all sentient beings and dependent upon the kindness and generosity of sponsors in order to do so. If you would like to make a donation to Wisdom, you may do so through our website or our Somerville office. If you would like to help sponsor the publication of a book, please write or email us at the address above.

Thank you.

Wisdom is a nonprofit, charitable 501(c)(3) organization affiliated with the Foundation for the Preservation of the Mahayana Tradition (FPMT).

THE WISDOM OF LISTENING
Edited by Mark Brady
320 pages, ISBN 0-86171-355-9 $16.95

"A very helpful anthology of 19 essays with sections on the promise, the practice, and the power of listening. Among the contributors are spiritual teacher Ram Dass; Marshall Rosenberg, founder of the Center for Nonviolent Communication; Anne Simpkinson, an editor for *Prevention* magazine; Kathleen Dowling Singh, a therapist and workshop leader; and Rodney Smith, director of the Hospice of Seattle. Their suggestions, perspectives, and practices will reinforce your intentions to be a good listener."—*Spirituality and Health*

THE NEW SOCIAL FACE OF BUDDHISM
A Call to Action
Ken Jones
Foreword by Kenneth Kraft
320 pages, ISBN 0-86171-365-6, $16.95

"In this substantially revised update of his *Social Face of Buddhism*, Jones argues that Buddhism has powerful, practical implications for profound social change. This is a meticulous, philosophical foundation for compassionate social action and a clear, attentive, thorough explication of the social-action implications of Buddhist thought."—*Publishers Weekly*

THE GREAT AWAKENING

A Buddhist Social Theory
David R. Loy
240 pages, ISBN 0-86171-366-4, $16.95

"Can we create policies that diminish or inhibit our negative tendencies and encourage the positive? David Loy, Zen teacher, social activist, and professor, skillfully entertains such issues, and offers ways of seeing that can help us make saner policies and recognize the bias in our institutions. The wisdom in this book's pages deserves a wide audience."—*Green Living*

CONFLICT, CULTURE, CHANGE

Engaged Buddhism in a Globalizing World
Sulak Sivaraksa
Foreword by Donald Swearer
160 pp, ISBN 0-86171-498-9, $14.95

From Nobel Peace Prize nominee Sulak Sivaraksa comes this look at Buddhism's innate ability to help change life on the global scale. *Conflict, Culture, Change* explores the cultural and environmental impacts of consumerism, nonviolence, and compassion, giving special attention to the integration of mindfulness and social activism, the use of Buddhist ethics to confront structural violence, and globalization's meaning in terms of traditional identity.